Excel

ADVANCED SKILLS

ENGLISH

YEAR 3

AGES 8–9

ADVANCED ENGLISH

Get the Results You Want!

PASCAL PRESS

Donna Gibbs

Contents

Introduction

The aim of the ***Excel*** **Advanced Skills: Advanced English** series is to build on and extend students' skills in English. Each book in the series supports the requirements of the Australian Curriculum (English) at each year level.

The series consists of six books, one for each year level, from Year 1 to Year 6. The series is supported by other books in the ***Excel*** **Advanced Skills English** range.

Structure of the book

Each book in the series contains:

- thirty carefully graded, three-page units of teaching and learning activities.
  - **Unit A** includes a sample informative, imaginative or persuasive text and deals with **Reading and comprehension skills**.
  - **Unit B** deals with the Conventions of language: **Spelling**, **Vocabulary**, **Grammar** and **Punctuation**.
  - **Unit C** deals with **Texts in context**. It provides for a deeper analysis and evaluation of the language choices authors make and the ways that readers make meaning from texts.
- four double-page NAPLAN-style tests.
- answers for all questions.

How to use this book

- Students should complete one unit per week. A suggested plan would be to complete the week's Unit A and B page on one day and the Unit C page on another day of the same week.
- After successfully completing a set of units (e.g. 1–7, 8–15, 16–23, 24–30), students should undertake the corresponding NAPLAN-style test.

How to use this book with the *Excel* Advanced Skills: Advanced Mathematics series

For a complete **weekly English and Mathematics program**, use this book in conjunction with the ***Excel*** **Advanced Skills: Year 3 Advanced Mathematics** book. This way a student will have work set for four days a week: two days for English and two days for Mathematics.

How to assess students' progress

- Templates are included in each book of the series that outline the knowledge and skills targeted by the questions in that book. (Please see page 6.)
- The questions move through the subtopics of English in exactly the same order in each book but as there are more questions and more complex material included in later years of the Year 1 to Year 6 continuum, the question numbers vary across the books.
- The results of the work undertaken in Units A and B can be recorded on the marking grid. See ways to use the marking grid on page 4.

Excel Advanced Skills titles

If students are having difficulty in any area, further support is available in other ***Excel*** workbooks. Please see the comprehensive list on page 5.

The *Excel* step-by-step improvement plan

Step 1

Read the introduction on page 3.

Step 2

Read the text below, along with the further explanation about the question templates and marking grids, on pages 6 and 7.

- **Question templates**

  These outline the knowledge and skills targeted by the questions in this book. Remember that the questions move through the subtopics of English in exactly the same order.

- **Marking grids**

  The results of the work undertaken in Units A and B can be recorded on the marking grid. This is an easy-to-use diagnostic tool that indicates each student's strengths and weaknesses in relation to specific areas of English.

  These results can be used to gather extra information about each student's progress and revision needs. For example, see the sample marking grid for Reading and comprehension in the right-hand column:

  - When marking answers on the grid, simply mark incorrect answers with 'X' in the appropriate box. This will result in a graphical representation of areas needing further work. An example for the first five units is shown above. If a question has several parts, it should be counted wrong if one or more mistakes are made.
  - Remember that you can identify exactly what type of questions a student is having difficulty with in a topic. For example, in the grid above the student is having difficulty with Reading and comprehension evaluative questions.
  - There is no marking grid for Unit C.

Marking grid

Reading and comprehension	Literal	Literal	Inferring	Inferring	Evaluative	Evaluative
Question	1	2	3	4	5	6
Unit 1						
Unit 2						X
Unit 3						
Unit 4						X
Unit 5						X
Unit 6						
Unit 7						
Unit 8						
Unit 9						
Unit 10						

This grid indicates that the student needs extra help and practice in evaluative questions.

Step 3

Refer to page 5: ***Excel* books to help you *get the results you want*!**

- Under each topic there is a list of books in our range to help students. Each ***Excel*** book has a comprehensive contents page that will help you find the appropriate pages in the book to target the specific topic you want in each subject area.

Excel books to help you *get the results you want!*

Reading and comprehension

Excel Advanced Skills

9781741254525

Excel NAPLAN*-style Tests

9781741253634

Excel NAPLAN*-style Tests

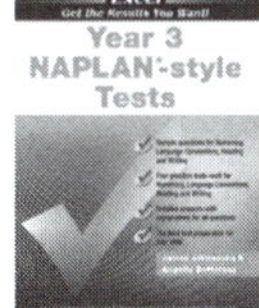

9781741251722

Spelling

Excel Advanced Skills

9781741252606

Excel Handbooks & Guides

9781864410617

Excel PRIMARY SPELLING HANDBOOK

9781741252637

Excel NAPLAN*-style Tests

9781741253634

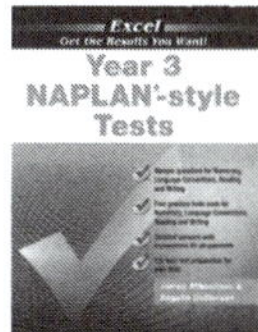

9781741251722

Vocabulary

Excel Advanced Skills

9781741252606

Excel NAPLAN*-style Tests

9781741253634

Excel NAPLAN*-style Tests

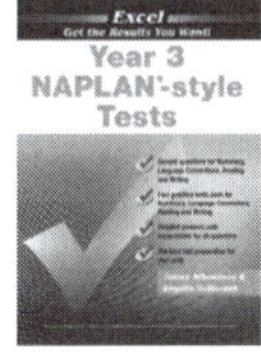

9781741251722

Grammar

Excel Advanced Skills

9781741254013

Excel Handbooks & Guides

9781864410600

Excel NAPLAN*-style Tests

9781741253634

Excel NAPLAN*-style Tests

9781741251722

Punctuation

Excel Advanced Skills

9781741253993

Excel NAPLAN*-style Tests

9781741253634

Excel NAPLAN*-style Tests

9781741251722

Writing

Excel Advanced Skills

9781741253993

Excel NAPLAN*-style Tests

9781741253634

Excel NAPLAN*-style Tests

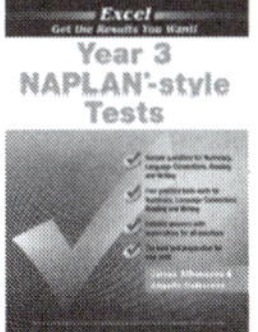

9781741251722

Question templates

Reading and comprehension

Q1–2 Literal: Answers to these questions are found directly in the text.

Q3–4 Inferring: Answers to these questions need to be worked out from clues in the text.

Q5–6 Evaluative: Answers to these questions rely on making judgements about information in the text and beyond the text.

Spelling

Q1–4 Misspelt words: In these questions, students use their understanding of spelling patterns and spelling rules to correct the spelling mistakes.

Q5 Word families: In this question, students use their understanding of base words, morphemes, prefixes, suffixes and etymology to create word families.

Vocabulary

Q6–7 Synonyms: In these questions, students need to comprehend the meanings of words in context.

Q8 Meaning in context/Word usage: This question requires students to use their knowledge of word meanings and usage to select an appropriate word from the text to complete a sentence.

Q8 Definitions: In this question, students are required to demonstrate understanding of word meanings and usage in the context of the text.

Q10–11 Antonyms: In these questions, students need to understand similarities and differences of word meanings.

Grammar

Q12 Nouns/Noun groups: This question deals with types of noun, e.g. concrete and abstract, and noun groups including articles, adjectives and pronouns.

Q13 Verbs/Verb groups: This question deals with aspects of a verb group, e.g. singular and plural, tense, subject–verb agreement and types of verbs.

Q14 Adverbials: This question deals with adverbials, e.g. prepositional phrases that tell when, where and how; and adverbs that modify and intensify.

Q15 Cohesion: This question deals with words that stand for other words, e.g. pronouns, and words that link clauses, e.g. conjunctions.

Punctuation

Q16–18 These questions deal with ways of punctuating sentences, e.g. adding capital letters, full stops, question marks, exclamation marks, commas, quotation marks and apostrophes.

Texts in context

Note: There is no marking grid for Unit C questions.

Q1–6 These questions deal with aspects of text, including:

Purpose and audience: These questions require students to recognise the purpose of a text (such as to inform, persuade or entertain) and the nature of its intended audience (the reader, listener or viewer).

Text structures and features: These questions require students to examine the ways a text is organised through, for example, sequencing, paragraphing and cohesive devices.

Textual interpretations: These questions help students to analyse and compare texts and evaluate their effectiveness through, for example, language choices, imagery and point of view.

Get creative

Q7 These tasks require students to create their own texts by adding to or responding to the models provided. Student responses will vary as these tasks are open-ended.

This icon indicates where students will need to use their own paper to answer the question.

Marking grid

Reading and comprehension	Literal	Literal	Inferring	Inferring	Evaluative	Evaluative
Question	1	2	3	4	5	6
Unit 1						
Unit 2						
Unit 3						
Unit 4						
Unit 5						
Unit 6						
Unit 7						
Unit 8						
Unit 9						
Unit 10						
Unit 11						
Unit 12						
Unit 13						
Unit 14						
Unit 15						
Unit 16						
Unit 17						
Unit 18						
Unit 19						
Unit 20						
Unit 21						
Unit 22						
Unit 23						
Unit 24						
Unit 25						
Unit 26						
Unit 27						
Unit 28						
Unit 29						
Unit 30						
Question	1	2	3	4	5	6

Marking grid

Conventions of language	Spelling					Vocabulary						Grammar				Punctuation		
	Misspelt words	Misspelt words	Misspelt words	Misspelt words	Word families	Synonyms	Synonyms	Meaning in context / Word usage	Definitions	Antonyms	Antonyms	Nouns / Noun groups	Verbs / Verb groups	Adverbials	Cohesion	Punctuation	Punctuation	Punctuation
Question	1	2	3	4	5	6	7	8	9	10	11	12	13	14	15	16	17	18
Unit 1																		
Unit 2																		
Unit 3																		
Unit 4																		
Unit 5																		
Unit 6																		
Unit 7																		
Unit 8																		
Unit 9																		
Unit 10																		
Unit 11																		
Unit 12																		
Unit 13																		
Unit 14																		
Unit 15																		
Unit 16																		
Unit 17																		
Unit 18																		
Unit 19																		
Unit 20																		
Unit 21																		
Unit 22																		
Unit 23																		
Unit 24																		
Unit 25																		
Unit 26																		
Unit 27																		
Unit 28																		
Unit 29																		
Unit 30																		
Question	1	2	3	4	5	6	7	8	9	10	11	12	13	14	15	16	17	18

Best of all

I like bridges.
I like cars.
I like eating
chocolate bars.

I don't like greens.
I don't like bullies.
I don't like hats
or wearing woollies

I do like school.
Is that a surprise?
I like playing football
and hot meat pies.

I don't like measles.
I don't like mumps.
I don't like chicken pox
With its itchy, red bumps!

I like computers;
I'm a bit of a fan.
But my favourite is
a story from Gran.

I'm off now to bed
'cos my list is complete.
Gran says that she hopes
my dreams will be sweet!

© Donna Gibbs

1. The poet does **not** like
   A cars. **B** greens. **C** school.

2. The poet likes
   A mumps. **B** bridges. **C** hats.

3. Choose **two** answers. Everyone would agree with the poet's opinion about
   A measles. **B** school. **C** chicken pox.

4. Choose **two** answers. Some people would disagree with the poet's opinion about
   A computers. **B** wearing woollies. **C** bullies.

5. The poet is .... about what she likes and dislikes.
   A certain **B** unsure **C** confused

6. In your opinion, which is the most unexpected like or dislike?

....

....

....

....

Answers and explanations on page 106

SPELLING

Write the correct spelling of the underlined words in questions 1–4.

1 My brother had the meezles last year.

2 What are you waring to the football?

3 Blue is my favorit colour.

4 I am saving some choclet for later.

5 Write three words from the word family that includes **surprise**.

VOCABULARY

Circle the answers in questions 6–7 that have the nearest meaning to the underlined words.

6 My list is complete.
- A finished
- B perfect
- C endless
- D reached

7 These are a few of my favourite things.
- A admired
- B popular
- C best-liked
- D pleasant

8 Add a word from the text to the sentence.

.... are their own worst enemies.

9 Write a word from the text to match the meaning.

an enthusiastic supporter ....

Circle the word that does **not** belong.

10
- A dislike
- B loathe
- C approve
- D hate

11
- A munching
- B feeding
- C chewing
- D chomping

GRAMMAR

12 Complete the sentence with a concrete noun from the text.

I like eating hot meat ....

13 Which form of the verb completes the sentence correctly?

I like to .... to the football.
- A went
- B goes
- C go
- D going

14 Write a prepositional phrase from the text that tells **where**.

Now I've written my list, I am going

....

15 Which pronoun refers to the underlined noun group? Write it in the sentence below.

He	She	It	You	They	I	We

My gran tells the best stories.

.... knows hundreds of them!

PUNCTUATION

Rewrite the sentences correctly.

16 i dont like cold winter mornings

17 did you get a surprise

18 im off to bed now

Answers and explanations on page 106

Best of all

I like bridges.
I like cars.
I like eating
chocolate bars.

I don't like greens.
I don't like bullies.
I don't like hats
or wearing woollies

I do like school.
Is that a surprise?
I like playing football
and hot meat pies.

I don't like measles.
I don't like mumps.
I don't like chicken pox
With its itchy, red bumps!

I like computers;
I'm a bit of a fan.
But my favourite is
a story from Gran.

I'm off now to bed
'cos my list is complete.
Gran says that she hopes
my dreams will be sweet!

1 'Best of all' is a poem that
- **A** describes the poet's life.
- **B** expresses the poet's opinions.
- **C** instructs people about how to behave.

2 The question (line 11) in the poem is a way of
- **A** connecting with the reader.
- **B** showing the poet's fears.
- **C** displaying the poet's knowledge.

3 Why doesn't the poet list all her likes first?
- **A** The contrast of likes and dislikes adds interest to the poem.
- **B** She listed things exactly as she thought of them.
- **C** She didn't think of doing it that way.

4 You can tell the poet is a girl because
- **A** she doesn't like chicken pox.
- **B** she doesn't like bullies.
- **C** the photo shows her with her gran.

5 Why is there an apostrophe before the word **'cos**?
- **A** to show to whom the list belongs
- **B** to show letters have been left out of the word
- **C** to show the poet wasn't sure how to spell the word

6 Would you like to have the poet as a friend? Why or why not?

....

....

....

....

7 Write your own poem entitled 'Best of all' using the text as a model.

Answers and explanations on page 106

Salties

Saltwater crocodiles, or 'salties' as Australians call them, live in the tropical areas of northern Australia. Their name suggests they live in salt water yet they also inhabit rivers, creeks and wetlands. They can also move about on land.

Saltwater crocodiles are the world's largest living reptiles. They have webbed feet and a long, muscular tail with flattened sides. Their eyes and nostrils are on the top of their broad snouts. They have powerful jaws containing 66 large teeth that can regrow when broken. This happens about 800 times in a lifetime. They eat small reptiles, turtles and fish but also large animals such as wild pigs, cattle, buffalo—and even humans!

The female lays about 50 eggs in a nest built from mud and vegetation. When the eggs hatch, she carries the babies to the water in her mouth. Only about one per cent of these survive to become adults.

1. Salties is another name for
   A freshwater crocodiles. **B** saltwater crocodiles. **C** baby crocodiles.

2. Saltwater crocodiles have
   A muscular tails. **B** short tails. **C** flat tails.

3. The shape of the crocodile's tail helps it to
   A cover its young while they hatch.
   B run quickly on land.
   C propel itself through the water.

4. Choose **two** answers. Having nostrils on top of its snout allows a crocodile to
   A keep most of its body hidden under the water.
   B see what is coming towards it.
   C breathe air.

5. Why do saltwater crocodiles need large teeth that regrow?
   A to attack and eat small reptiles
   B to attack and eat large animals
   C to make their jaws powerful

6. What is the most likely reason so few crocodiles reach adulthood?

Answers and explanations on page 106

SPELLING

Write the correct spelling of the underlined words in questions 1–4.

1 Freshwater crockodials don't swim in the sea. ....

2 They live in troppical areas.

....

3 Its nostrills are on top of its snout.

....

4 How many babies will sirvive?

....

5 Write three words from the word family that includes **built**.

....

....

VOCABULARY

Circle the answers in questions 6–7 that have the nearest meaning to the underlined words.

6 Salties can regrow broken teeth.

A sore B mangled
C damaged D crushed

7 Nests are made from mud and vegetation.

A plants B vegetables
C flowers D fronds

8 Add a word from the text to the sentence.

Saltwater crocodiles .... fresh water as well as salt water.

9 Write a word from the text to match the meaning.

land that has wet, spongy soil such as a marsh, swamp or bog ....

Circle the word or word group that does **not** belong.

10 A live B dwell
C survive D inhabit

11 A happens B stops
C occurs D takes place

GRAMMAR

12 Complete the sentence with a concrete noun from the text.

The .... hatch after about three months.

13 Which form of the verb completes the sentence correctly?

Female salties .... their eggs in a well-hidden nest.

A lay B lays
C is laying D has laid

14 Write a prepositional phrase from the text that tells **where**.

Their name suggests they live

....

15 Which pronoun refers to the underlined noun group? Write it in the sentence below.

he	she	it	you	they	I	we

The female crocodile makes a nest

before .... lays her eggs.

PUNCTUATION

Rewrite the sentences correctly.

16 they visit rivers streams and wetlands

....

....

17 they eat wild pigs cattle buffaloes and humans

....

....

18 when the eggs are ready to hatch the babies chirp

....

....

Answers and explanations on page 106

Salties

Saltwater crocodiles, or 'salties' as Australians call them, live in the tropical areas of northern Australia. Their name suggests they live in salt water yet they also inhabit rivers, creeks and wetlands. They can also move about on land.

Saltwater crocodiles are the world's largest living reptiles. They have webbed feet and a long, muscular tail with flattened sides. Their eyes and nostrils are on the top of their broad snouts. They have powerful jaws containing 66 large teeth that can regrow when broken. This happens about 800 times in a lifetime. They eat small reptiles, turtles and fish but also large animals such as wild pigs, cattle, buffalo—and even humans!

The female lays about 50 eggs in a nest built from mud and vegetation. When the eggs hatch, she carries the babies to the water in her mouth. Only about one per cent of these survive to become adults.

1 What is the purpose of this text?
   - **A** to explain what crocodiles look like
   - **B** to warn people to keep well away from crocodiles
   - **C** to provide information about saltwater crocodiles

2 Where would you be likely to find this text?
   - **A** in a school magazine
   - **B** in a book about reptiles
   - **C** in a newspaper article about a crocodile attack

3 Which of the following statements could be added to paragraph two?
   - **A** Their stomachs are small so they sometimes wedge their prey in branches.
   - **B** Saltwater crocodiles also live in New Guinea and South-East Asia.
   - **C** The babies make a tweeting noise when they are ready to hatch.

4 The word salties is different from the other words in the text because
   - **A** it is a typical Australian abbreviation.
   - **B** it is a scientific term.
   - **C** it names something imaginary.

5 The author's attitude to the subject of crocodiles is
   - **A** fearful and worried.
   - **B** matter of fact.
   - **C** full of admiration.

6 The Queensland government has a 'crocwise' campaign to educate people about crocodiles. Why do you think a campaign is needed?

....

....

....

....

....

....

Get creative

7 Research the freshwater crocodile. List three differences between freshwater and saltwater crocodiles.

Answers and explanations on page 107

READING AND COMPREHENSION

My wish list

Dear Tom and Alisa

I know you look after me quite well. But there are ways you could improve. I have made a wish list of how I'd like you to change.

1 When you see a notice that says 'NO DOGS, PLEASE', ignore it. It means don't let any other dogs in. You can safely take me anywhere as I always behave well.

2 Learn to talk dog talk, please. Only yesterday, on our walk, I asked you to go into the butcher's shop to get me a bone. You didn't! And you didn't even answer me! If you could bark, whine, whimper and growl we'd understand each other much better.

3 You know how I let you sleep in my bed at night, Tom? Well, I would be very grateful if you wouldn't move about and kick at the bedclothes. It disturbs my dreams.

With much doggy love
Will

1 How many items are on Will's wish list?
A one **B** two **C** three

2 What does the notice say?
A DOGS NOT ALLOWED **B** NO DOGS, PLEASE **C** KEEP OUT, DOGS

3 Why wouldn't Tom and Alisa agree to item 1?
A They could be breaking the law.
B They want to punish Will for his bad behaviour.
C They aren't sure if Will's argument makes sense.

4 Why wouldn't Tom agree to item 3? Choose **two** answers.
A It is Tom's bed, not Will's.
B Tom doesn't want Will to sleep on his bed.
C Tom can't control his limbs when he is asleep.

5 There is evidence that Tom and Alisa
A are cruel to Will. **B** look after Will well. **C** need to be kinder to Will.

6 What would Will's owners think of his letter to them?

....

....

Answers and explanations on page 107

SPELLING

Write the correct spelling of the underlined words in questions 1–4.

1. Will is quiet well-behaved.

2. I wish you would anser me.

3. I'd be most greatful if you'd do that.

4. The dog gave a little wimper.

5. Write three words from the word family that includes **understand**.

VOCABULARY

Circle the answers in questions 6–7 that have the nearest meaning to the underlined words.

6. You need to improve the way you care for me!
   - A make better
   - B revise
   - C alter
   - D increase

7. Please don't ignore what I say.
   - A lose
   - B repeat
   - C forget
   - D remember

8. Add a word from the text to the sentence.

   Tom decided to write a list of ways Will could ……………………… .

9. Write a word from the text to match the meaning.

   interferes with; interrupts ………………………

Circle the word that does **not** belong.

10.
   - A rejected
   - B pleased
   - C thankful
   - D grateful

11.
   - A correctly
   - B carefully
   - C safely
   - D carelessly

GRAMMAR

12. Complete the sentence with a concrete noun from the text.

    You have kicked the ……………………… off the bed!

13. Which form of the verb completes the sentence correctly?

    I ……………… a wish list yesterday morning.
    - A make
    - B makes
    - C made
    - D had made

14. Write a prepositional phrase from the text that tells **where**.

    I asked you to go ……………………… .

15. Which pronoun refers to the underlined noun group? Write it in the sentence below.

he	she	it	you	they	I	we

    Tom and Alisa said ……………………… will reply to my letter.

PUNCTUATION

Rewrite the sentences correctly.

16. dont let your dogs inside our gate

17. will you visit the butchers shop

18. id like you to change some of your ways please

Answers and explanations on page 107

My wish list

Dear Tom and Alisa

I know you look after me quite well. But there are ways you could improve. I have made a wish list of how I'd like you to change.

1 When you see a notice that says 'NO DOGS, PLEASE', ignore it. It means don't let any other dogs in. You can safely take me anywhere as I always behave well.

2 Learn to talk dog talk, please. Only yesterday, on our walk, I asked you to go into the butcher's shop to get me a bone. You didn't! And you didn't even answer me! If you could bark, whine, whimper and growl we'd understand each other much better.

3 You know how I let you sleep in my bed at night, Tom? Well, I would be very grateful if you wouldn't move about and kick at the bedclothes. It disturbs my dreams.

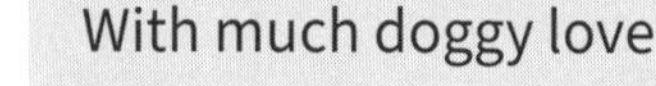

With much doggy love
Will

1 The purpose of this text is to
- **A** instruct.
- **B** entertain.
- **C** report.

2 What makes Will's letter amusing?
- **A** Dogs don't write letters.
- **B** Tom and Alisa can't read.
- **C** The reader can't speak dog language.

3 How is the text organised?
- **A** a letter inside a list
- **B** a list inside a letter
- **C** a list followed by a letter

4 Will's complaints are
- **A** fair.
- **B** ridiculous.
- **C** reasonable.

5 Which of these would **not** make a good title for the text?
- **A** Do dogs think?
- **B** What next!
- **C** Will takes charge

6 Who is the dog in the picture?
- **A** Will hoping to be let inside the gate
- **B** a friend of Will's who wishes he was inside the gate with Will
- **C** a dog that has nothing to do with Will

7 Add item number four to Will's wish list.

Answers and explanations on page 107

READING AND COMPREHENSION

Forgotten Giants

The Forgotten Giants, a group of six sculptures, can be found hidden in out-of-the-way places in Copenhagen, the capital city of Denmark. Thomas Dambo is the sculptor who created them. He used only recycled materials and worked with local volunteers at sites he chose carefully.

It was his idea to hide the giants in places not often visited. At first, people thought this was foolish but soon their opinions changed.

Hill Top Trine has big hands. You can climb up into them for a wonderful view of the surrounding area. Sleeping Louis, who sleeps on a hillside, has a mouth you can crawl inside. Little Tilde stands looking through the trees at a small lake. She has 28 birdhouses inside her wooden body! And Teddy Friendly stands by a stream with a long arm outstretched to help people cross over.

Photo reproduced with kind permission of Thomas Dambo

Maybe you will visit Copenhagen one day to see them for yourself.

1. Which sculpture has a mouth you can climb inside?
   - **A** Hill Top Trine
   - **B** Sleeping Louis
   - **C** Little Tilde

2. Which sculpture has bird houses inside her body?
   - **A** Little Tilde
   - **B** Hill Top Trine
   - **C** Teddy Friendly

3. What is the name of the sculpture in the photo?
   - **A** Sleeping Louis
   - **B** Teddy Friendly
   - **C** Hill Top Trine

4. Choose **two** answers. The Forgotten Giants are placed
   - **A** in the natural world.
   - **B** in out-of-the way-places.
   - **C** where they can be easily found.

5. Why did people's opinions change? (lines 5–6)
   - **A** The sculptures had plenty of space.
   - **B** The out-of-the-way places became popular as people visited.
   - **C** Thomas Dambo wouldn't change his mind.

6. What is most unusual about Thomas Dambo's sculptures?

   ....

   ....

Answers and explanations on pages 107–108

SPELLING

Write the correct spelling of the underlined words in questions 1–4.

1 These giants are made from resikaled materials. ....

2 Have you seen the Forgoten Giants?

....

3 Little Tilde has a large woodden body.

....

4 Teddy Friendly's arm is outstreched.

....

5 Write three words from the word family that includes **visit.**

....

VOCABULARY

Circle the answers in questions 6–7 that have the nearest meaning to the underlined words.

6 It wasn't a foolish idea after all.
- A weak
- B feeble
- C silly
- D insane

7 I have only seen four of the group of sculptures.
- A collection
- B crowd
- C gang
- D band

8 Add a word from the text to the sentence.

Thomas Dambo .... recycled materials to create his Forgotten Giants.

9 Write a word from the text to match the meaning.

used again, usually in a different way

....

Circle the word that does **not** belong.

10
- A changed
- B destroyed
- C altered
- D shifted

11
- A naps
- B sleeps
- C awakens
- D snoozes

GRAMMAR

12 Complete the sentence with a concrete noun from the text.

If you climb into Hill Top Trine's

.... you can see far and wide.

13 Which form of the verb completes the sentence correctly?

Do you think you .... the Forgotten Giants one day?
- A visit
- B visited
- C have visited
- D will visit

14 Write a prepositional phrase from the text that tells **where**.

Little Tilde has 28 birdhouses hidden

....

15 Which pronoun refers to the underlined noun group? Write it in the sentence below.

he	she	it	you	they	I	we

The sculptures are well hidden so

.... are hard to find.

PUNCTUATION

Rewrite the sentences correctly.

16 you need a map to find the forgotten giants

....

....

17 I climbed all over hill top trine

....

....

18 copenhagen is the capital of Denmark

....

....

Answers and explanations on page 108

TEXTS IN CONTEXT

Forgotten Giants

The Forgotten Giants, a group of six sculptures, can be found hidden in out-of-the-way places in Copenhagen, the capital city of Denmark. Thomas Dambo is the sculptor who created them. He used only recycled materials and worked with local volunteers at sites he chose carefully.

It was his idea to hide the giants in places not often visited. At first, people thought this was foolish but soon their opinions changed.

Hill Top Trine has big hands. You can climb up into them for a wonderful view of the surrounding area. Sleeping Louis, who sleeps on a hillside, has a mouth you can crawl inside. Little Tilde stands looking through the trees at a small lake. She has 28 birdhouses inside her wooden body! And Teddy Friendly stands by a stream with a long arm outstretched to help people cross over.

Photo reproduced with kind permission of Thomas Dambo

Maybe you will visit Copenhagen one day to see them for yourself.

1 The purpose of this text is to
- **A** provide instructions about how to find the giants.
- **B** give information about some unusual sculptures.
- **C** persuade people to visit Copenhagen.

2 The photograph is useful for
- **A** seeing the size of the giant.
- **B** seeing the giant in close-up.
- **C** seeing what big hands the giant has.

3 How can you tell Thomas Dambo is fond of the natural world?
- **A** He made six different sculptures.
- **B** He places his giants where people can enjoy nature.
- **C** He named his giants after volunteers.

4 Why does the name Little Tilde make you smile?
- **A** She sounds like a happy giant.
- **B** It makes you wonder if there is a Big Tilde.
- **C** She is called 'Little' but she is an enormous giant.

5 What do the giant's names have in common?
- **A** They all include a person's name.
- **B** They all begin with a person's name.
- **C** They all end with a person's name.

6 How are the Forgotten Giants different from fairytale giants? (If you haven't read any fairytales with giants in them, you may need to do so before you answer this.)

7 Design a new Forgotten Giant to add to the group. List the materials you would use to make it. Give your giant a name and say where you would like it to be placed.

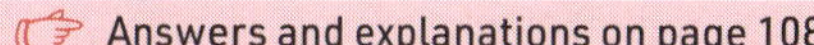
Answers and explanations on page 108

Mother's Day

Dear Diary

It's Mother's Day tomorrow. Harry and I are going to make a special afternoon tea for Mum. We plan to serve tea and coffee with fruit and custard tarts made by us. Dad has said he'll stand by in the kitchen in case we need help. (Harry always spills things. Brothers can be such a nuisance, dear Diary!)

We have bought some ready-made pastry cases and some strawberries. Tomorrow we'll need to make the custard. Here is the recipe for the custard:

Ingredients

2 eggs
3 tbs cornflour
3 cups milk
3 tbs sugar
1 tsp vanilla essence

Method

Put eggs, cornflour and milk into a saucepan and whisk until smooth.
Place on a medium heat and keep whisking until it becomes a creamy custard.
Take from the heat. Whisk in sugar and vanilla.

Wish me luck. I'll let you know how it all goes tomorrow.

Love
Vivienne

1 How much milk is needed for the recipe?
A one cup **B** two cups **C** three cups

2 What did they buy that was ready-made?
A pastry cases **B** custard **C** strawberries

3 How many people will be at the afternoon tea?
A two **B** four **C** six

4 Choose **two** answers. The children will need to
A pour the custard into the pastry cases.
B turn on the oven.
C top the custard with chopped strawberries.

5 Why does Harry spill things?
A He is still quite little. **B** He is very naughty. **C** He likes annoying Vivienne.

6 Do you think the Mother's Day afternoon tea will be a success?

Answers and explanations on page 108

SPELLING

Write the correct spelling of the underlined words in questions 1–4.

1 What will you do on Muthers Day?

2 We plan to cook the custard toomrow.

3 Be careful not to spil that!

4 Wisk it until it is creamy, please.

5 Write three words from the word family that includes **luck**.

VOCABULARY

Circle the answers in questions 6–7 that have the nearest meaning to the underlined words.

6 My brother can be a nuisance sometimes.
- A disaster
- B bother
- C mess
- D shame

7 I always write in my diary at night.
- A regularly
- B continually
- C endlessly
- D forever

8 Add a word from the text to the sentence.

Yesterday we .... strawberries at the supermarket.

9 Write a word from the text to match the meaning.

the time between noon and evening

Circle the word that does **not** belong.

10
- A smooth
- B velvety
- C creamy
- D lumpy

11
- A assistance
- B harm
- C aid
- D help

GRAMMAR

12 Complete the sentence with a concrete noun from the text.

.... are my favourite fruit.

13 Which form of the verb completes the sentence correctly?

We .... tea and coffee tomorrow.
- A serve
- B served
- C will serve
- D have served

14 Write a prepositional phrase from the text that tells **where**.

Put eggs and milk ....

15 Which pronoun refers to the underlined noun group? Write it in the sentence below.

he	she	it	you	they	I	we

I get annoyed with my brother when .... spills things.

PUNCTUATION

Rewrite the sentences correctly.

16 its mothers day tomorrow

17 dad says hell be there if we need help

18 whisk the eggs flour and milk together

Answers and explanations on page 108

Mother's Day

Dear Diary

It's Mother's Day tomorrow. Harry and I are going to make a special afternoon tea for Mum. We plan to serve tea and coffee with fruit and custard tarts made by us. Dad has said he'll stand by in the kitchen in case we need help. (Harry always spills things. Brothers can be such a nuisance, dear Diary!)

We have bought some ready-made pastry cases and some strawberries. Tomorrow we'll need to make the custard. Here is the recipe for the custard:

Ingredients

2 eggs
3 tbs cornflour
3 cups milk
3 tbs sugar
1 tsp vanilla essence

Method

Put eggs, cornflour and milk into a saucepan and whisk until smooth.
Place on a medium heat and keep whisking until it becomes a creamy custard.
Take from the heat. Whisk in sugar and vanilla.

Wish me luck. I'll let you know how it all goes tomorrow.

Love
Vivienne

1. The purpose of this diary entry is mainly to
   - **A** record personal thoughts.
   - **B** exchange recipe information.
   - **C** summarise important events.

2. What type of text is the recipe inside the diary?
   - **A** a discussion
   - **B** a recount
   - **C** a procedure

3. Why is the comment about Harry in brackets?
   - **A** to draw attention to its importance
   - **B** to separate it from Vivienne's plans for the event
   - **C** to show Vivienne doesn't like Harry

4. When is it likely this photograph was taken?
   - **A** the day before Mother's Day
   - **B** on Mother's Day
   - **C** the day after Mother's Day

5. Vivienne treats her diary as
   - **A** a friend.
   - **B** a parent.
   - **C** a teacher.

6. What does the photograph add to your understanding of the text? 

7. Write a diary entry in which you describe how you plan to get ready for a celebration of your choice.

Answers and explanations on pages 108–109

READING AND COMPREHENSION

That's not cricket

Once upon a time there were three brothers: Big Bully, Bigger Bully and Biggest Bully. They liked to frighten children in the nearby park.

On Sunday morning, Harry and Rose were in the park playing cricket. Big Bully was there too. He loved cricket. When Rose hit a six, Big Bully ran and got the ball. He threw it back. He looked on longingly.

'Would you like to play with us?' Harry called.

Big Bully nodded. He hoped his bigger brothers wouldn't see him.

When it was Big Bully's turn to bat, the ball sailed over the trees and landed in the front yard of the Bullys' house.

Bigger Bully rushed headlong into the park, a menacing look on his face.

'Would you like to play too?' asked Rose as he skidded to a halt in front of her.

No-one had ever smiled at him like that. And he did love cricket!

'You can bowl,' said Harry.

'Two down, one to go,' Harry whispered triumphantly to Rose.

1. Where were Harry and Rose playing cricket?
   - **A** in the park
   - **B** over the trees
   - **C** in the Bullys' front yard

2. What did Rose hit?
   - **A** Big Bully
   - **B** a six
   - **C** a bat

3. Why did Big Bully hope his brothers wouldn't see him?
   - **A** He was hiding from them.
   - **B** He wasn't behaving like a bully.
   - **C** He thought they'd want to play too.

4. Why did Bigger Bully have a menacing look on his face?
   - **A** He always had a menacing look on his face.
   - **B** He was angry with his brother.
   - **C** He wanted to punish the person who'd hit the ball into his yard.

5. 'Two down, one to go' (line 15). Who is the 'one to go'?
   - **A** Rose
   - **B** Biggest Bully
   - **C** Big Bully

6. Why were Harry and Rose feeling triumphant?

....

....

Answers and explanations on page 109

SPELLING

Write the correct spelling of the underlined words in questions 1–4.

1 How many chilldrin were in the park?

2 He rushed heddlong towards me!

3 The ball saled over the trees.

4 'We won,' they cried tryumfantly.

5 Write three words from the word family that includes **frighten**.

VOCABULARY

Circle the answers in questions 6–7 that have the nearest meaning to the underlined words.

6 He looked at them longingly.
A gladly B thirstily
C sadly D enviously

7 The ball sailed high in the sky.
A soared B skimmed
C reached D went

8 Add a word from the text to the sentence.
Big Bully rushed towards her then ________ to a stop.

9 Write a word from the text to match the meaning.
said very softly using more breath than voice

Circle the word that does **not** belong.

10 A distant B nearby
C far D faraway

11 A arrived B landed
C left D settled

GRAMMAR

12 Complete the sentence with a concrete noun from the text.
He hit the ball over the ________.

13 Which form of the verb completes the sentence correctly?
Rose ________ kindly at Biggest Bully then handed him the ball.
A smiles B smiled
C had smiled D is smiling

14 Write a prepositional phrase from the text that tells **where**.
The three bullies frightened children ________.

15 Which pronoun refers to the underlined noun group? Write it in the sentence below.

he	she	it	you	they	I	we

Biggest Bully bowled the ball.
________ hit the stumps!

PUNCTUATION

Rewrite the sentences correctly.

16 would you like to play asked Harry

17 the bullys house was nearby

18 thats what happened

Answers and explanations on page 109

That's not cricket

Once upon a time there were three brothers: Big Bully, Bigger Bully and Biggest Bully. They liked to frighten children in the nearby park.

On Sunday morning, Harry and Rose were in the park playing cricket. Big Bully was there too. He loved cricket. When Rose hit a six, Big Bully ran and got the ball. He threw it back. He looked on longingly.

'Would you like to play with us?' Harry called.

Big Bully nodded. He hoped his bigger brothers wouldn't see him.

When it was Big Bully's turn to bat, the ball sailed over the trees and landed in the front yard of the Bullys' house.

Bigger Bully rushed headlong into the park, a menacing look on his face.

'Would you like to play too?' asked Rose as he skidded to a halt in front of her.

No-one had ever smiled at him like that. And he did love cricket!

'You can bowl,' said Harry.

'Two down, one to go,' Harry whispered triumphantly to Rose.

1 What is the purpose of this text?

- **A** to give instructions
- **B** to tell a story
- **C** to report an event

2 The narrator is

- **A** a character involved in the action.
- **B** one of the bullies.
- **C** someone outside of the action.

3 Which answer describes the structure of the text?

- **A** a sequence of arguments and evidence
- **B** a point of view with supporting reasons
- **C** orientation, complication, resolution

4 Choose **two** answers. The Bullys' names refer to

- **A** how much they eat.
- **B** how much bullying they do.
- **C** their different sizes.

5 The title, 'That's not cricket', means

- **A** it is unfair, or not playing the game, to bully.
- **B** cricket is an unfair game.
- **C** playing cricket always solves everyone's problems.

6 Could the events in the text happen in the real world? Why or why not?

....

....

....

....

....

....

Get creative

7 Continue the story for another ten lines.

Answers and explanations on page 109

READING AND COMPREHENSION

Fact file: the platypus

The platypus:

- is a native Australian monotreme (a type of mammal that lays eggs).
- has a bill and webbed feet like a duck's, a tail like a beaver's and a body and brown fur like an otter's. (In 1799, when British scientists first saw a preserved platypus, they thought it had been made by stitching parts of different animals together as a trick!)
- is semiaquatic and inhabits small streams and rivers.
- paddles with its front feet and steers with its back feet and tail.
- has a bill that senses electric fields caused by movement. It uses it to search for, and scoop up, insects, worms and shellfish from the bottom of river beds.
- has spurs on its heels that can sting predators. The male's sting is venomous.
- has webbing on its feet that retracts to expose claws. Claws are used when building a burrow on a riverbank or when running on land.

1. The sting of the .... platypus is venomous.
   A male and female **B** female **C** male
2. The platypus steers with its
   A front feet. **B** back feet and its tail. **C** back feet.
3. A female platypus
   A gives birth to live babies. **B** lays eggs. **C** hatches eggs inside her body.
4. Choose **two** answers. The bill of the platypus is useful because
   A it guides it towards its prey.
   B it can dig down for, and scoop up, prey.
   C it acts like an extra tail.
5. What does semiaquatic mean?
   A lives on land
   B lives in water
   C lives partly on land and partly in water
6. What makes the platypus's appearance unusual?

....

....

Answers and explanations on page 109

SPELLING

Write the correct spelling of the underlined words in questions 1–4.

1 Is the platypus a mamal? ……………………

2 Scyentists thought someone was playing a trick on them. ……………………

3 Monotreams usually lay their eggs in nests. ……………………

4 The platipuss can retract the webbing on its feet. ……………………

5 Write three words from the word family that includes **brown**.

……………………

……………………

VOCABULARY

Circle the answers in questions 6–7 that have the nearest meaning to the underlined words.

6 The platypus can scoop up worms with its bill.

A bulldoze	B toss
C dig	D sift

7 Its tail is used to steer its body through water.

A direct	B send
C float	D move

8 Add a word from the text to the sentence.

They …………………… it was made by stitching parts of animals together!

9 Write a word from the text to match the meaning.

born in a particular place or country

……………………

Circle the word that does **not** belong.

10

A shows	B reveals
C displays	D hides

11

A venomous	B poisonous
C deadly	D helpful

GRAMMAR

12 Complete the sentence with a concrete noun from the text.

A platypus has a …………………… rather like a duck's.

13 Which form of the verb completes the sentence correctly?

When scientists …………………… it, they couldn't believe their eyes.

A sees	B see
C seen	D saw

14 Write a prepositional phrase from the text that tells **where**.

It builds its burrow …………………… .

15 Which pronoun refers to the underlined noun group? Write it in the sentence below.

he she it you they I we

The platypus spends a lot of time swimming. …………………… needs this time to hunt for its food.

PUNCTUATION

Rewrite the sentences correctly.

16 the males sting can make humans ill

……………………

……………………

17 its tail is like a beavers

……………………

……………………

18 they thought it was a trick

……………………

……………………

Answers and explanations on pages 109–110

Fact file: the platypus

The platypus:

- is a native Australian monotreme (a type of mammal that lays eggs).
- has a bill and webbed feet like a duck's, a tail like a beaver's and a body and brown fur like an otter's. (In 1799, when British scientists first saw a preserved platypus, they thought it had been made by stitching parts of different animals together as a trick!)
- is semiaquatic and inhabits small streams and rivers.
- paddles with its front feet and steers with its back feet and tail.
- has a bill that senses electric fields caused by movement. It uses it to search for, and scoop up, insects, worms and shellfish from the bottom of river beds.
- has spurs on its heels that can sting predators. The male's sting is venomous.
- has webbing on its feet that retracts to expose claws. Claws are used when building a burrow on a riverbank or when running on land.

1. What is the purpose of the text?
   - **A** to explain what makes the platypus unusual
   - **B** to present information about the platypus
   - **C** to discuss the habits of the platypus
2. What connects the dot points in the text?
   - **A** They are about what the platypus looks like.
   - **B** They are about what the platypus can do.
   - **C** They give general information about the platypus.
3. The vocabulary includes a number of
   - **A** technical terms.
   - **B** poetic ideas.
   - **C** biased opinions.
4. Why is the sentence beginning '(In 1799, …' (line 5) in brackets?
   - **A** to express great surprise
   - **B** to show it isn't the same kind of information
   - **C** to stress its importance
5. Another suitable title for this text would be
   - **A** Monotremes.
   - **B** Mammals.
   - **C** The duck-billed platypus.
6. Read the poem 'Old Man Platypus' by Banjo Paterson. (You can find it online at, for example, http://gutenberg.net.au/ebooks06/0603441h.html#06/.) What does the poet think platypuses look like when they are asleep?

Get creative

7. Choose three different animals. Create a new animal by combining parts from each of them. Draw and label your creation. Add three dot points that give information about it.

Answers and explanations on page 110

Wonka the wonder dog

'That dog is useless,' Hilary said.

'Yes, Billy. Couldn't you have chosen something bigger than a Chihuahua?' asked Tim.

'There's nothing wrong with Wonka,' Billy replied huffily.

A few weeks later Billy and his friends were playing in an old shed at the bottom of the paddock near Tim's house. When they were ready to leave, they found the doors had stuck. They wouldn't budge and the window was way too small for them to squeeze through. Except for Wonka. She fitted easily enough.

'Go, Wonka. Fetch Dad,' Billy cried.

Wonka took off fast. She had to burrow under the broken fence paling and then bark at the door until Billy's dad came out.

After the imprisoned children were rescued, Billy's friends sang a different tune!

'Well done, Wonka,' said Hilary.

'What a brilliant dog,' added Tim.

Billy thought of saying 'I told you so' but instead he just patted Wonka lovingly.

1 The wonder dog is named

- **A** Billy.
- **B** Hilary.
- **C** Tim.
- **D** Wonka.

2 Where did Billy and his friends play a few weeks later?

- **A** in a paddock
- **B** in an old shed
- **C** at Hilary's house
- **D** beside the broken fence

3 Why does Billy reply 'huffily'? (line 4)

- **A** He has a cold.
- **B** He and his dog have been insulted.
- **C** His friends made him laugh.
- **D** He can't get his breath.

4 How does Billy feel about his dog? Choose **all** that apply.

- **A** embarrassed by her
- **B** bonded to her
- **C** disappointed in her
- **D** proud of her

5 What does 'sang a different tune' (line 14) mean?

- **A** changed their opinion
- **B** sang out of tune
- **C** changed the song they were singing
- **D** sang in chorus

6 Why doesn't Billy say 'I told you so'? (line 17)

- **A** He's too tired to say anything.
- **B** He heard his father say it.
- **C** He doesn't want to rub it in.
- **D** He knows it won't prove he was right.

7 What does the picture add to the text?

....

....

....

....

Answers and explanations on page 110

Each sentence has one word that is incorrect. Write the correct spelling of each word.

1 I heard a dog houling loudly last night.

....

2 Willy pressed hard agenst the fence to get through.

....

3 It hapened after they were rescued.

....

4 I don't think they were lissening to what I said.

....

Read the text below. Choose the correct word or word group to complete the sentences.

The choice

I looked at Great Danes, Chihuahuas ....(5).... Fox Terriers at the dog shelter. It ....(6).... easy to choose ....(7).... Wonka stared at me with her big ....(8).... eyes.

5 A but B and C with D for

6 A was B will be C weren't D were

7 A although B because C before D during

8 A browner B brownest C brown D BROWN

9 Which word is a noun in this sentence?

He thought my idea was fantastic.

A He
B thought
C idea
D fantastic

10 Which word correctly completes the sentence?

.... you choose your dog, you are allowed to take it home.

A Whether
B Until
C While
D After

11 Choose the correct word to complete the sentence.

Billy's friends thought he'd chosen badly. .... were quite rude about his dog.

A We
B They
C He
D You

12 Which words tell **where**?

They said Wonka had lived at the dog shelter for ages.

A They said
B had lived
C at the dog shelter
D for ages

13 Which sentence has the apostrophe in the correct place?

A Its' raining today.
B Do you think I've got that right?
C The clock has it's hands pointing to midday.
D Have'nt you got any pets at all?

14 Which sentence is punctuated correctly?

A My dog is the best dog ever!
B My dog is the best dog ever.
C My dog is the best dog ever?
D My dog is the bes't dog ever!

Answers and explanations on page 110

READING AND COMPREHENSION

Goodbye plastic bags?

You're listening to 3RY FM: the radio station that keeps you up-to-date.

Remember that book from your childhood with the holes in its pages? Yep! *The Very Hungry Caterpillar* by Eric Carle. It was about a caterpillar who ate everything in its path. And it's a fact: as a caterpillar prepares to become a butterfly, it eats an enormous amount—up to tens of thousands of times its body weight. Yikes!

Now comes the good news. Yesterday morning scientists announced they have discovered a tiny caterpillar called a waxworm that can eat through plastic at extremely high speeds. They hope to use this knowledge to learn how to get rid of the large amounts of plastic that litter our world.

Plastic bags (about 4 million of them are used in Australia each year) pollute oceans, rivers and the environment. They take forever to break down and they kill thousands of marine animals and seabirds. It's a problem worth solving, so fingers crossed!

1. What is 3RY FM?
   - **A** a place
   - **B** a radio station
   - **C** a book
2. How many plastic bags are used in Australia each year?
   - **A** about 4 million
   - **B** trillions
   - **C** about 4 billion
3. Why is the speed at which waxworms eat plastic important?
   - **A** because scientists are in a hurry
   - **B** because nothing else has been able to get rid of plastic quickly
   - **C** because plastic bags take forever to break down
4. What makes the news 'good' (line 8)? Choose **two** answers.
   - **A** There's hope a difficult problem will be solved.
   - **B** Waxworms can eat through plastic quickly.
   - **C** The lives of many animals and birds may be saved.
5. Why is the title a question?
   - **A** because no-one is sure the problem will go away
   - **B** to show the announcer is raising her voice
   - **C** because plastic bags can't answer back
6. How many stars would you give this radio broadcast out of five? Explain your reasons.

Answers and explanations on page 110

SPELLING

Write the correct spelling of the underlined words in questions 1–4.

1 Caterpillars eat many times their body wait.

....

2 Are you lissening to 3RY FM?

....

3 Waxworms eat at extreamly high speeds.

....

4 Plastic bags polute our oceans.

....

5 Write three words from the word family that includes **prepares**.

....

VOCABULARY

Circle the answers in questions 6–7 that have the nearest meaning to the underlined words.

6 The waxworm is a tiny caterpillar.

A young B unformed
C babyish D small

7 Plastic bags pollute our environment.

A climate B surroundings
C background D place

8 Add a word from the text to the sentence.

There are a few weeks when a caterpillar .... to become a butterfly.

9 Write a word from the text to match the meaning.

something that needs a solution ....

Circle the word that does **not** belong.

10 A foul B infect
C pollute D cleanse

11 A enormous B medium-sized
C gigantic D huge

GRAMMAR

12 Complete the sentence with an abstract noun from the text.

Scientists will be able to make good use of their new ....

13 Which form of the verb completes the sentence correctly?

Scientists .... their discovery on the radio yesterday.

A announce B will announce
C announcing D announced

14 Write a prepositional phrase from the text that tells **when**.

They reported the news ....

15 Which pronoun refers to the underlined noun group? Write it in the sentence below.

he	she	it	you	they	I	we

We avoid plastic bags because .... cause so much harm.

PUNCTUATION

Rewrite the sentences correctly.

16 have you read *the very hungry caterpillar*

....

17 that book had holes in its pages

....

18 plastic pollutes oceans rivers and the environment

....

Answers and explanations on pages 110–111

Goodbye plastic bags?

You're listening to 3RY FM: the radio station that keeps you up-to-date.

Remember that book from your childhood with the holes in its pages? Yep! *The Very Hungry Caterpillar* by Eric Carle. It was about a caterpillar who ate everything in its path. And it's a fact: as a caterpillar prepares to become a butterfly, it eats an enormous amount—up to tens of thousands of times its body weight. Yikes!

Now comes the good news. Yesterday morning scientists announced they have discovered a tiny caterpillar called a waxworm that can eat through plastic at extremely high speeds. They hope to use this knowledge to learn how to get rid of the large amounts of plastic that litter our world.

Plastic bags (about 4 million of them are used in Australia each year) pollute oceans, rivers and the environment. They take forever to break down and they kill thousands of marine animals and seabirds. It's a problem worth solving, so fingers crossed!

1 What is the main purpose of this broadcast?
- **A** to remind people of a book
- **B** to report a discovery
- **C** to tell Australians to stop using plastic bags

2 Who is the audience for this broadcast?
- **A** scientists
- **B** children
- **C** the general public

3 Why is a children's book mentioned?
- **A** to make a connection with the listener
- **B** to keep the audience up-to-date
- **C** to fill in time before getting to the point

4 What evidence is there that this text is spoken? Choose **two** answers.
- **A** It talks directly to the listener.
- **B** It uses formal, scientific vocabulary.
- **C** It includes slang and casual expressions.

5 The broadcaster delivers the news
- **A** in a friendly, chatty way.
- **B** in a nervous, shy way.
- **C** in a dull, plain way.

6 The broadcaster's point of view about the discovery is
- **A** unclear.
- **B** optimistic.
- **C** pessimistic.

Get creative

7 Listen to an item from a news broadcast on the radio. Write down two ways it is different from 'Goodbye plastic bags?'

Answers and explanations on page 111

READING AND COMPREHENSION

Mascots

Good morning, 3 Blue.

A mascot is a person, animal or thing thought to bring good luck. For example, Wally is the mascot of the Australian national rugby union team, the Wallabies.

In 2000 the mascots chosen for the Sydney Olympics were Syd, a duck-billed platypus; Olly, a kookaburra; and Millie, an echidna. The committee said they'd decided to avoid koalas and kangaroos!

Even so, Borobi, the surfing koala, was chosen to be the mascot for the 2018 Gold Coast Commonwealth Games. Borobi is a very special and unique koala—he is missing the second thumb on each paw, which makes it difficult to climb trees. Named after the Yugambeh word for koala, Borobi's paws have Indigenous markings.

Another well-known mascot is Sid the seagull who wears board shorts, a t-shirt and a hat. He has promoted Cancer Council's Slip-Slop-Slap campaign since the 1980s. This encourages people to cover up and stay out of the sun.

Thank you.

1 What is the name of the Wallabies mascot?

A Sid **B** Borobi **C** Wally

2 In which year were the Sydney Olympics held?

A 2000 **B** 2018 **C** 1980

3 Why might koalas and kangaroos have been avoided?

A Nobody likes them anymore. **B** They are difficult to recognise. **C** They are too well-known.

4 Choose **two** answers. The Sydney Olympics' mascots

A are examples of Australian fauna.
B are large concrete figures.
C represent water, air and earth.

5 Why does Sid the seagull wear clothes?

A to make him stand out
B to remind people to cover up in the sun
C to make him look Australian

6 Do you think Borobi is a good choice of mascot? Why or why not?

....

....

Answers and explanations on page 111

SPELLING

Write the correct spelling of the underlined words in questions 1–4.

1 The name of the mascot, Syd, refers to Sidney.

....

2 The name of the mascot, Olly, refers to the Ollympics. ....

3 Millie, the ekidna, has a name that refers to the millennium.

....

4 Borobi's paws have Indidgenous markings.

....

5 Write three words from the word family that includes **climb**.

....

VOCABULARY

Circle the answers in questions 6–7 that have the nearest meaning to the underlined words.

6 Borobi has one thumb missing from each paw.

A mislaid B unknown
C elsewhere D absent

7 That mascot is well known in the football community.

A familiar B ordinary
C popular D unaccepted

8 Add a word from the text to the sentence.

The committee .... it didn't want a kangaroo as its mascot this time.

9 Write a word from the text to match the meaning.

a planned series of actions with a particular purpose ....

Circle the word that does **not** belong.

10 A avoid B skip
C allow D dodge

11 A prevents B permits
C hinders D forbids

GRAMMAR

12 Complete the sentence with an abstract noun from the text.

We think our mascot will bring us good .... this year.

13 Which form of the verb completes the sentence correctly?

What did the committee .... about the new mascot?

A say B says
C said D saying

14 Write a prepositional phrase from the text that tells **when**.

The Sydney Olympics were held ....

15 Which pronoun refers to the underlined noun group? Write it in the sentence below.

he	she	it	you	they	I	we

'Which animal mascot do .... like, Mary?'

PUNCTUATION

Rewrite the sentences correctly.

16 a person animal or thing can be a mascot

....

....

17 in 2000 olly was a mascot for the olympics

....

....

18 sid wears shorts a t-shirt and a hat

....

....

Answers and explanations on page 111

Mascots

Good morning, 3 Blue.

A mascot is a person, animal or thing thought to bring good luck. For example, Wally is the mascot of the Australian national rugby union team, the Wallabies.

In 2000 the mascots chosen for the Sydney Olympics were Syd, a duck-billed platypus; Olly, a kookaburra; and Millie, an echidna. The committee said they'd decided to avoid koalas and kangaroos!

Even so, Borobi, the surfing koala, was chosen to be the mascot for the 2018 Gold Coast Commonwealth Games. Borobi is a very special and unique koala—he is missing the second thumb on each paw, which makes it difficult to climb trees. Named after the local Indigenous Yugambeh word for 'koala', Borobi's paws have Indigenous markings.

Another well-known mascot is Sid the seagull who wears board shorts, a t-shirt and a hat. He has promoted Cancer Council's Slip-Slop-Slap campaign since the 1980s. This encourages people to cover up and stay out of the sun.

Thank you.

1. What is the purpose of this text?
   - **A** to explain how to choose a mascot
   - **B** to give information about mascots
   - **C** to give reasons why mascots are useful

2. Where would you hear this text?
   - **A** in a classroom
   - **B** on talkback radio
   - **C** on television

3. Which of these lines makes clear this is a spoken text?
   - **A** The committee said they'd decided to avoid koalas and kangaroos!
   - **B** This encourages people to cover up and stay out of the sun.
   - **C** Good morning, 3 Blue.

4. The named mascots are mainly linked to
   - **A** sporting events.
   - **B** health campaigns.
   - **C** sporting teams.

5. Why are the mascots given abbreviated names?
   - **A** They can be said quickly.
   - **B** They sound more formal.
   - **C** It is an Australian habit to abbreviate the names of popular figures.

6. Give some reasons why people have mascots.

   ....

   ....

   ....

Get creative

7. Prepare a talk that gives information about mascots in a culture other than Australia (e.g. China, Japan, the USA).

Answers and explanations on page 111

READING AND COMPREHENSION

Little Frog in the well

Once there was a little frog who lived at the bottom of an old well. He had water to drink, insects to eat and a rock to rest on. Sometimes a passing bird would stop and chat.

'Come down and play with me,' said the frog.

'No, thank you. It's much better up here,' replied the bird.

'Nowhere could be better than here,' said the frog.

The birds grew fed up with the frog's stubborn attitude. The yellow sparrow grew particularly angry when the frog, for the seventh time, refused its offer to show the frog the outside world.

One day, in exasperation, the sparrow flew into the well, picked up the frog and put him on its back. The frog was amazed to see the world's magnificent mountains and sparkling seas. He asked to be put down so he could explore and admire all the wonders that were before him. Funnily enough, he never returned to his old home!

(This is a retelling of a folk story from Taiwan.)

1 Where was the frog's home?

A on a rock **B** in some water **C** in a well

2 What did the frog eat?

A sparrows **B** insects **C** birds

3 Why did the frog refuse the sparrow's invitations?

A He thought his well was better than anywhere else.
B He didn't like the yellow sparrow.
C He thought the sparrow wanted to eat him.

4 Why did the birds get annoyed? Choose **two** answers.

A They felt they knew better than the frog.
B The frog was foolishly stubborn.
C They wanted to have him for their dinner.

5 The frog's attitude changed from

A dislike to love. **B** belief to annoyance. **C** disbelief to astonishment.

6 Why didn't the frog return to his old home?

....

....

Answers and explanations on page 112

SPELLING

Write the correct spelling of the underlined words in questions 1–4.

1 Frogs include insexts in their diet.

....

2 'Im going nowhair,' said the frog.

....

3 What was the frog's atitude to life in the well?

....

4 The mountens were spread out beneath them. ....

5 Write three words from the word family that includes **refuse**.

....

....

VOCABULARY

Circle the answers in questions 6–7 that have the nearest meaning to the underlined words.

6 I like to rest on the rock in my well.

A relax **B** sleep
C pause **D** wait

7 He was a very stubborn frog.

A short-sighted **B** obstinate
C difficult **D** contrary

8 Add a word from the text to the sentence.

The frog changed his .... when he saw the world outside his well.

9 Write a word from the text to match the meaning.
state of being extremely annoyed

....

Circle the word or word group that does **not** belong.

10 **A** delved into **B** explored
C overlooked **D** examined

11 **A** refused **B** denied
C permitted **D** rejected

GRAMMAR

12 Complete the sentence with an abstract noun from the text.

The sparrow's .... was understandable.

13 Which form of the verb completes the sentence correctly?

I didn't think the frog .... all he saw, did you?

A admires **B** will admire
C is admiring **D** would admire

14 Write a prepositional phrase from the text that tells **when**.

.............................., the sparrow felt so angry that he went and got the frog.

15 Which pronoun refers to the underlined noun group? Write it in the sentence below.

he	she	it	you	they	I	we

The birds were cross because .... thought the frog was being stubborn.

PUNCTUATION

Rewrite the sentences correctly.

16 will you play with me asked the frog

....

....

17 strangely enough he lived happily ever after

....

....

18 no thank you replied the bird

....

....

Answers and explanations on page 112

Little Frog in the well

Once there was a little frog who lived at the bottom of an old well. He had water to drink, insects to eat and a rock to rest on. Sometimes a passing bird would stop and chat.

'Come down and play with me,' said the frog.

'No, thank you. It's much better up here,' replied the bird.

'Nowhere could be better than here,' said the frog.

The birds grew fed up with the frog's stubborn attitude. The yellow sparrow grew particularly angry when the frog, for the seventh time, refused its offer to show the frog the outside world.

One day, in exasperation, the sparrow flew into the well, picked up the frog and put him on its back. The frog was amazed to see the world's magnificent mountains and sparkling seas. He asked to be put down so he could explore and admire all the wonders that were before him. Funnily enough, he never returned to his old home!

(This is a retelling of a folk story from Taiwan.)

1 What is the purpose of this text?
- **A** to describe the life cycle of a frog
- **B** to persuade people to be kind to frogs
- **C** to tell a story about a frog

2 Who is the narrator?
- **A** the storyteller
- **B** the frog
- **C** the yellow sparrow

3 What action triggers an important change?
- **A** the swallow flying the frog out of the well
- **B** the frog refusing the sparrow's offer
- **C** the frog feeling content with his lot

4 Why are the words 'Funnily enough' (line 13) included?
- **A** The tale is really a funny joke.
- **B** The frog had a sense of humour.
- **C** What happens is the opposite of what the frog expected.

5 What is the moral of this folk story?
- **A** It is wise to be kind.
- **B** It is unwise to close your mind to new things.
- **C** It pays to trust everyone.

6 What are the frog's strengths and weaknesses?

....

....

....

....

....

....

Get creative

7 Practise retelling this story aloud in your own words. When you feel you are ready, perform it for an audience.

Answers and explanations on page 112

FLIGHTS	**HOLIDAY PACKAGES**	WHAT'S ON	SUBSCRIBE	ABOUT US	CONTACT US

Fortnight of Fun

Does your family have the travel bug? We at **Trend Travel** have the solution. The **Fortnight of Fun** Travel Package.

This fourteen-day tour of Japan is full of opportunities for family fun. Fast trains, breathtaking beauty, fabulous food. What are you waiting for?

Ask today about our sensationally low-priced package. You'll enjoy every moment.

For starters, you and your family will:

- travel on a high-speed bullet train (up to 320 km an hour)
- visit Miyajima, known as the Island of Gods, famous for its floating shrine
- see Japan's sacred deer when the cherry blossoms are blooming in springtime
- cycle beside rice fields and through charming rural scenery
- learn how to make a paper lantern
- learn to play a traditional Taiko drum
- see Aibo, the robotic dog, in action.

Don't delay. Call today before this magical package disappears.

1 The Fortnight of Fun is
A an advertisement. **B** a travel package. **C** a tour.

2 What is Miyajima?
A a shrine **B** a God **C** an island

3 Which phrase is **not** an opinion?
A fast trains **B** breathtaking scenery **C** fabulous food

4 Choose **two** answers. The Fortnight of Fun
A doesn't include activities. **B** is suitable for adults. **C** is suitable for children.

5 The joke that the magical package might disappear (line 19) is used
A to encourage the viewer to act quickly.
B to make the viewer suspicious.
C to convince the viewer the package really is magical.

6 Do you think this is an effective advertisement? Why or why not?

....

....

Answers and explanations on page 112

SPELLING

Write the correct spelling of the underlined words in questions 1–4.

1 We have the solootion to your problem.

....

2 Mount Fuji looked brethtakeing in the sunshine. ....

3 We shall visit an ireland while we are there.

....

4 I've never seen such beautiful seenery.

....

5 Write three words from the word family that includes **cycle**.

....

....

VOCABULARY

Circle the answers in questions 6–7 that have the nearest meaning to the underlined words.

6 It is such a low-priced package!
- A reduced
- B inexpensive
- C cut-rate
- D slashed

7 It has a famous floating shrine.
- A fabulous
- B grand
- C well-known
- D splendid

8 Add a word from the text to the sentence.

If you ...., you could miss out altogether!

9 Write a word from the text to match the meaning.

programmed to do jobs usually done by a person ....

Circle the word that does **not** belong.

10
- A amazing
- B breathtaking
- C puzzling
- D astonishing

11
- A magical
- B enchanting
- C spellbinding
- D spooky

GRAMMAR

12 Complete the sentence with an abstract noun from the text.

The .... of the scenery took my breath away.

13 Which form of the verb completes the sentence correctly?

I am going to .... every moment of this holiday.
- A enjoyed
- B had enjoyed
- C enjoy
- D enjoying

14 Write a prepositional phrase from the text that tells **when**.

The cherry blossoms come into bloom

....

15 Which pronoun refers to the underlined noun group? Write it in the sentence below.

he	she	it	you	they	I	we

My sister told me that .... wants to go to Japan.

PUNCTUATION

Rewrite the sentences correctly.

16 fast trains breathtaking beauty fantastic food

....

....

17 will you buy the fortnight of fun package today

....

....

18 aibo the robotic dog is very popular

....

....

Answers and explanations on page 112

FLIGHTS | **HOLIDAY PACKAGES** | WHAT'S ON | SUBSCRIBE | ABOUT US | CONTACT US

Fortnight of Fun

Does your family have the travel bug? We at **Trend Travel** have the solution. The **Fortnight of Fun** Travel Package.

This fourteen-day tour of Japan is full of opportunities for family fun. Fast trains, breathtaking beauty, fabulous food. What are you waiting for?

Ask today about our sensationally low-priced package. You'll enjoy every moment.

For starters, you and your family will:

- travel on a high-speed bullet train (up to 320 km an hour)
- visit Miyajima, known as the Island of Gods, famous for its floating shrine
- see Japan's sacred deer when the cherry blossoms are blooming in springtime
- cycle beside rice fields and through charming rural scenery
- learn how to make a paper lantern
- learn to play a traditional Taiko drum
- see Aibo, the robotic dog, in action.

Don't delay. Call today before this magical package disappears.

1 This webpage persuades people to
   - **A** learn more about Japan.
   - **B** travel to Japan.
   - **C** buy the Fortnight of Fun travel package.

2 Who is the target audience?
   - **A** trendy groups
   - **B** teenagers
   - **C** families

3 What information would you find if you clicked on the words 'ABOUT US'?
   - **A** personal information about people who made the website
   - **B** information about Trend Travel
   - **C** information about other travel packages

4 If you were to click on the words 'CONTACT US', how would they change?
   - **A** They would disappear.
   - **B** They would move their place in the line.
   - **C** They would become bold.

5 Which claim is **not** made in the advertisement?
   - **A** The Fortnight of Fun package offers value for money.
   - **B** It includes a range of activities to appeal to families.
   - **C** You will travel from one end of Japan to the other.

6 Which technique is **not** used in this advertisement?
   - **A** repetition to reinforce the message
   - **B** commands to tell you what to do
   - **C** appeals that tug at your heartstrings

7 Use the internet to find two more images that could be added to this webpage. Record their web addresses here.

Answers and explanations on page 113

How to have a garage sale

Our family had a successful garage sale at the weekend. Everyone got involved—Mum, Dad, my two sisters and me, Oliver.

I have made up a list of rules to follow for the next time:

1. Pick a date that doesn't clash with other local events.
2. Make posters to advertise our sale well in advance.
3. Gather items beforehand from everyone, including rellies and neighbours.
4. Sort things into categories such as shoes, books, kitchen utensils, toys.
5. Collect tables ready to display your items.
6. Get plenty of change from the bank. (We were worried when our first buyers only spent 25 cents and needed change from 20 dollars.)
7. Make a timetable for when each family member is on sales duty. (Amy and Fran quarrelled over this for ages, to my annoyance.)
8. Collect any leftovers so we can donate them to our nearby charity shop.

1 Who made up the list of rules?

A Mum **B** Dad **C** Oliver

2 How does Oliver suggest the sale should be advertised?

A have tables ready **B** make posters **C** make a timetable

3 Numbers 2 and 3 should be done

A on the day of the sale. **B** during the sale. **C** well before the sale.

4 Why should things be sorted into categories? Choose **two** answers.

A It makes it more fun.
B It makes it easier for buyers to see what is available.
C It makes it easier to find what you are looking for.

5 Which item definitely won't contribute to the success of the sale?

A 6 **B** 8 **C** 3

6 How would you describe Oliver?

....

....

Answers and explanations on page 113

SPELLING

Write the correct spelling of the underlined words in questions 1–4.

1 Was your garage sale sucksessful?

....

2 Where did you advurtize your sale?

....

3 Everrywon came to our sale!

....

4 The sisters quarelled about everything.

....

5 Write three words from the word family that includes **collect**.

....

....

VOCABULARY

Circle the answers in questions 6–7 that have the nearest meaning to the underlined words.

6 I am collecting the items that don't sell to give away.

A selecting B gathering
C hoarding D choosing

7 We sorted our sale items into different categories.

A types B levels
C divisions D compartments

8 Add a word from the text to the sentence.

We wanted to avoid .... events as they might take away our customers.

9 Write a word from the text to match the meaning.

show or exhibit ....

Circle the word that does **not** belong.

10 A beforehand B immediately
C sooner D earlier

11 A argued B quarrelled
C bickered D complained

GRAMMAR

12 Complete the sentence with an abstract noun from the text.

To my .... Amy and Fran lost some of the change.

13 Which form of the verb completes the sentence correctly?

We .... we wouldn't have enough change.

A worry B will worry
C were worried D are worrying

14 Write a prepositional phrase from the text that tells **when**.

We held our garage sale ....

....

15 Which pronoun refers to the underlined noun group? Write it in the sentence below.

he	she	it	you	they	I	we

Our garage sale was successful but

.... was pretty hard work.

PUNCTUATION

Rewrite the sentences correctly.

16 we sold books toys and clothes at our sale

....

....

17 everyone helped including mum dad and me

....

....

18 the date doesnt clash with mums birthday does it

....

....

Answers and explanations on page 113

How to have a garage sale

Our family had a successful garage sale at the weekend. Everyone got involved—Mum, Dad, my two sisters and me, Oliver.

I have made up a list of rules to follow for the next time:

1. Pick a date that doesn't clash with other local events.
2. Make posters to advertise our sale well in advance.
3. Gather items beforehand from everyone, including rellies and neighbours.
4. Sort things into categories such as shoes, books, kitchen utensils, toys.
5. Collect tables ready to display your items.
6. Get plenty of change from the bank. (We were worried when our first buyers only spent 25 cents and needed change from 20 dollars.)
7. Make a timetable for when each family member is on sales duty. (Amy and Fran quarrelled over this for ages, to my annoyance.)
8. Collect any leftovers so we can donate them to our nearby charity shop.

1 Oliver's list

A looks at different points of view.
B explains why things happen.
C tells how to do something.

2 What is Oliver's goal in writing his list?

A to make guidelines for future garage sales
B to reflect on past mistakes
C to give him something to do in the present

3 The first word in each list is an action verb that

A recalls a memory.
B gives an instruction.
C describes an activity.

4 Using a word like **rellies** makes Oliver sound

A less formal.
B more anxious.
C more distant.

5 Oliver uses brackets in his list

A to change the meaning of what he says.
B to add emphasis to what he argues.
C to separate comments that aren't strictly relevant.

6 Is Oliver's list-making a waste of time? Why or why not?

7 List three rules for how to plan a birthday party.

Answers and explanations on page 113

Triple zero

Triple zero is the phone number to ring in an emergency. An emergency is a serious, unexpected and often dangerous situation needing immediate action. By phoning triple zero you will be connected to someone who can send help. They can also advise about what to do while you are waiting for help to arrive.

The Australian government, along with Emergency services, has developed the Emergency+ app. This can be downloaded to a mobile phone. If a call is made from that phone to triple zero during an emergency then the location of the caller is able to be found more easily.

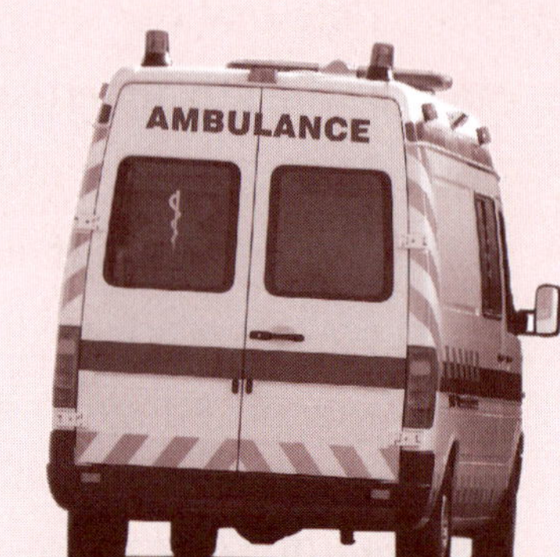

The Triple Zero Kids' Challenge is another app that helps children learn how to deal with a crisis such as a fire or when someone is badly injured.

Some children have earned the name Triple Zero Hero for their behaviour during an emergency.

1. Triple zero is
   - **A** an emergency.
   - **B** a phone number.
   - **C** an award.
2. Who made the Emergency+ app?
   - **A** the Australian government
   - **B** the Emergency services
   - **C** the Australian government and Emergency services
3. The Triple Zero Kids' Challenge was developed
   - **A** for adults to help children in emergencies.
   - **B** for children to learn more about what to do in an emergency.
   - **C** to make money for the government.
4. What kind of help could arrive after you ring Triple Zero? Choose **two** answers.
   - **A** meals-on-wheels
   - **B** an ambulance
   - **C** a fire engine
5. Triple Zero
   - **A** must only be dialled in real emergencies.
   - **B** can offer help about everything.
   - **C** must only be phoned by adults.
6. What kind of behaviour do you think should earn a child a Triple Zero Hero award?

....

....

Answers and explanations on pages 113–114

SPELLING

Write the correct spelling of the underlined words in questions 1–4.

1 The phone number is Tripple Zero.

....

2 It was an emurgancy! ....

3 The government has developped some helpful apps.

....

4 They were on their best behaveyour.

....

5 Write three words from the word family that includes **help**.

....

....

VOCABULARY

Circle the answers in questions 6–7 that have the nearest meaning to the underlined words.

6 The accident was unexpected.

A startling B eye-opening
C amazing D surprising

7 She was able to advise what to do on her phone.

A warn B recommend
C hear D mention

8 Add a word from the text to the sentence.

It is an app that can be .... to a phone.

9 Write a word from the text to match the meaning.

without any delay ....

Circle the word that does **not** belong.

10 A harmless B alarming
C dangerous D threatening

11 A injured B changed
C hurt D harmed

GRAMMAR

12 Complete the sentence with an abstract noun from the text.

He rang triple zero because there was an

....

13 Which form of the verb completes the sentence correctly?

Could you .... me what I should do next, please?

A have advised B advise
C advised D advising

14 Write a prepositional phrase from the text that tells **when**.

You should ring Triple Zero ....

....

15 Which pronoun refers to the underlined noun group? Write it in the sentence below.

he	she	it	you	they	I	we

My phone isn't working because .... has a faulty battery.

PUNCTUATION

Rewrite the sentences correctly.

16 is the emergency+ app helpful

....

....

17 a girl in our street was made a triple zero hero

....

....

18 what should you do in an emergency

....

....

Answers and explanations on page 114

Triple zero

Triple zero is the phone number to ring in an emergency. An emergency is a serious, unexpected and often dangerous situation needing immediate action. By phoning triple zero you will be connected to someone who can send help. They can also advise about what to do while you are waiting for help to arrive.

The Australian government, along with Emergency services, has developed the Emergency+ app. This can be downloaded to a mobile phone. If a call is made from that phone to triple zero during an emergency then the location of the caller is able to be found more easily.

The Triple Zero Kids' Challenge is another app that helps children learn how to deal with a crisis such as a fire or when someone is badly injured.

Some children have earned the name Triple Zero Hero for their behaviour during an emergency.

1. The purpose of the text is to
   - **A** provide entertainment.
   - **B** persuade people to buy something.
   - **C** inform people about preparing for an emergency.
2. The writer's attitude to the subject is
   - **A** serious.
   - **B** playful.
   - **C** a mixture of serious and playful.
3. The last line is included mainly to
   - **A** warn adults what is expected of their children.
   - **B** create a happy ending for the story.
   - **C** make people aware that children can handle emergencies.
4. The word app (software that can run on the internet) is an abbreviation for
   - **A** apple.
   - **B** application.
   - **C** appetite.
5. Another suitable title for the text would be
   - **A** Apps for emergencies.
   - **B** Locating that ambulance!
   - **C** Are you ready for an emergency?
6. What does a child need to do during an emergency to receive a Triple Zero Hero award?

7. Design a logo for Triple Zero.

Answers and explanations on pages 113–114

The Land of Nod' by RL Stevenson

From breakfast on through all the day
At home among my friends I stay,
But every night I go abroad
Afar into the land of Nod.

All by myself I have to go,
With none to tell me what to do —
All alone beside the streams
And up the mountain-sides of dreams.

The strangest things are there for me,
Both things to eat and things to see,
And many frightening sights abroad
Till morning in the land of Nod.

Try as I like to find the way,
I never can get back by day,
Nor can remember plain and clear
The curious music that I hear.

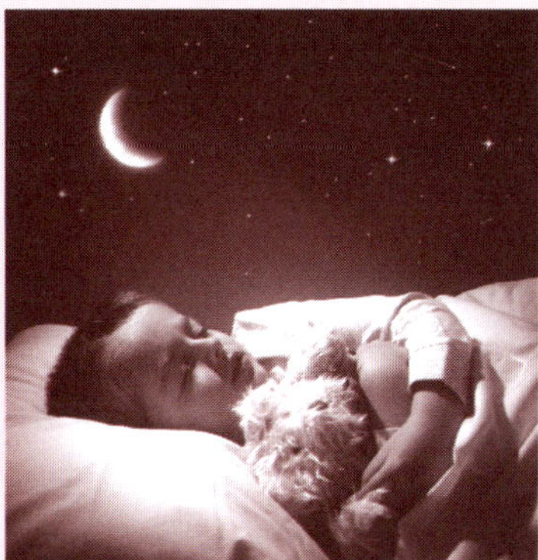

1. Where does the poet stay in the daytime?
   - **A** at school
   - **B** at play
   - **C** at home

2. How often does the poet visit the Land of Nod?
   - **A** now and then
   - **B** every night
   - **C** every day

3. What is the Land of Nod?
   - **A** the world of dreams
   - **B** a country similar to Australia
   - **C** a place overseas that you can visit

4. Choose **two** answers. The Land of Nod
   - **A** is a good place to hear music.
   - **B** has things in it familiar from the real world.
   - **C** is different from the real world in important ways.

5. Why does the poet go 'all alone' (line 8)?
   - **A** No-one else wants to go with him.
   - **B** He doesn't want anyone else with him.
   - **C** It is not possible to take someone where he is going.

6. How does the poet feel when he is in the Land of Nod?

   ....

   ....

Answers and explanations on page 114

SPELLING

Write the correct spelling of the underlined words in questions 1–4.

1 What did you have for brekfast?

....

2 I slept all thrugh the night.

....

3 The sights I saw were quite fritening to me.

....

4 I can remember hearing some cureious music. ....

5 Write three words from the word family that includes **remember**.

....

....

VOCABULARY

Circle the answers in questions 6–7 that have the nearest meaning to the underlined words.

6 I can't remember anything about my dream.

A revive B recall
C relive D reread

7 I saw some frightening sights.

A awful B grisly
C scary D grim

8 Add a word from the text to the sentence.

I .... to get back to the land of Nod in the daytime, but I never can.

9 Write a word from the text to match the meaning.

most unusual ....

Circle the word that does **not** belong.

10 A always B forever
C never D eternally

11 A many B lots
C numerous D few

GRAMMAR

12 Add an abstract noun to the sentence.

I sometimes have .... about strange places.

13 Which form of the verb completes the sentence correctly?

No-one is there to .... me what to do.

A told B telling
C tell D tells

14 Write a prepositional phrase from the text that tells **when**.

I go abroad ....

15 Which pronoun refers to the underlined noun group? Write it in the sentence below.

he	she	it	you	they	I	we

Robert Louis Stevenson said .... had lots of dreams as a child.

PUNCTUATION

Rewrite the sentences correctly.

16 i went to the land of nod all by myself

....

....

17 the poem was written by rl stevenson

....

....

18 the land of nod is a well-known poem

....

....

Answers and explanations on page 114

TEXTS IN CONTEXT

The Land of Nod' by RL Stevenson

From breakfast on through all the day
At home among my friends I stay,
But every night I go abroad
Afar into the land of Nod.

All by myself I have to go,
With none to tell me what to do —
All alone beside the streams
And up the mountain-sides of dreams.

The strangest things are there for me,
Both things to eat and things to see,
And many frightening sights abroad
Till morning in the land of Nod.

Try as I like to find the way,
I never can get back by day,
Nor can remember plain and clear
The curious music that I hear.

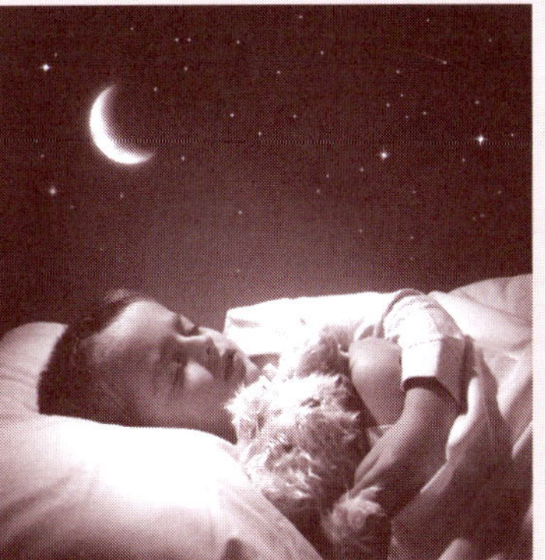

1 The purpose of this text is to
- **A** persuade people to recall their dreams.
- **B** share some personal experiences.
- **C** describe an adventure.

2 This text is likely to be found in
- **A** a book of adventures.
- **B** a book of poems.
- **C** a book about why people dream.

3 What would you think if the last verse was left out of the poem?
- **A** You would think the poet was afraid of his dreams.
- **B** You would think the poet forgot about his dreams in the day.
- **C** You would think the poet preferred night-time to daytime.

4 The rhymes in the text
- **A** add humour to the poem.
- **B** tie ideas closely together.
- **C** make the poem like a lullaby.

5 What makes the land of Nod seem like a real place?
- **A** It has things in it that are also in the real world.
- **B** You can always hear strange music there.
- **C** You have to go abroad to get there.

6 How well does the picture suit the poem?

....

....

....

....

....

Get creative

7 Write a verse about a dream you have had in which the first and second lines and the third and fourth lines rhyme.

Answers and explanations on pages 114–115

Dragonflies

The newborn dragonfly is wingless. It is coloured brown or green and blends with its surroundings. It spends most of its time under water. These nymphs are strongly predatory, mainly eating other insects.

After a year or more, the nymph leaves the water. Its outer skeleton cracks and an abdomen and wings emerge. The body of the adult dragonfly is often brightly coloured while its wings are transparent and embedded with tiny black veins. Each wing can be moved independently of the other.

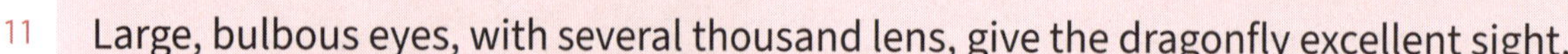

Large, bulbous eyes, with several thousand lens, give the dragonfly excellent sight. Dragonflies can detect a wider range of colours than humans.

Its forward-angled legs are used while in flight to grasp its prey. As a dragonfly can fly swiftly or hover, and fly in any direction including sideways or backwards, it has a talent for hunting. It devours an enormous number of flying insects, including mosquitoes.

1. Dragonfly nymphs mainly eat
   A frogs. **B** other insects. **C** mosquitoes.

2. An adult dragonfly has .... wings.
   A transparent **B** brightly coloured **C** dull

3. Dragonflies are helpful to humans because
   A they keep down the mosquito population.
   B they have veins in their wings.
   C their wings are transparent.

4. Which features of the dragonfly are likely to inspire the creation of new technology? Choose **two** answers.
   A its flight skills **B** its remarkable vision **C** its brightly coloured body

5. Why does a dragonfly sometimes look like a helicopter?
   A It can fly quickly. **B** It can detect movement. **C** It can hover in the air.

6. How similar are dragonfly nymphs and adults? Explain.

....

....

....

Answers and explanations on page 115

SPELLING

Write the correct spelling of the underlined words in questions 1–4.

1 Draggonflys can fly in all directions.

....

2 They blend with their surowndings.

....

3 Each eye has thowsands of facets.

....

4 Mosskitoes make a tasty meal.

....

5 Write three words from the word family that includes **detect**.

....

....

VOCABULARY

Circle the answers in questions 6–7 that have the nearest meaning to the underlined words.

6 The colouring blends with its surroundings.

A atmosphere B neighbourhood
C community D environment

7 Dragonflies can fly swiftly.

A hurriedly B quickly
C promptly D hastily

8 Add a word from the text to the sentence.

Black criss-crossed veins can be seen through their .... wings.

9 Write a word from the text to match the meaning.

hunts other animals for food ....

Circle the word that does **not** belong.

10 A detect B see
C view D hide

11 A grasp B hold
C release D clasp

GRAMMAR

12 Complete the sentence with an abstract noun from the text.

My .... is swimming.
What is yours?

13 Which form of the verb completes the sentence correctly?

Dragonflies .... to be excellent hunters.

A are said B are saying
C said D have said

14 Write a prepositional phrase from the text that tells **when**.

..........,
the nymph leaves its watery home.

15 Which pronoun refers to the underlined noun group? Write it in the sentence below.

he	she	it	you	they	I	we

Their eyes are extraordinary because
.... can see so many colours.

PUNCTUATION

Rewrite the sentences correctly.

16 a nymphs colours blend into its surroundings

....

....

17 its clear that a dragonfly is a talented insect

....

....

18 its eyes are large and bulb like

....

....

Answers and explanations on page 115

Dragonflies

❶ The newborn dragonfly is wingless. It is coloured brown or green and blends with its surroundings. It spends most of its time under water. These nymphs are strongly predatory, mainly eating other insects.

❷ After a year or more, the nymph leaves the water. Its outer skeleton cracks and an abdomen and wings emerge. The body of the adult dragonfly is often brightly coloured while its wings are transparent and embedded with tiny black veins. Each wing can be moved independently of the other.

❸ Large, bulbous eyes, with several thousand lens, give the dragonfly excellent sight. Dragonflies can detect a wider range of colours than humans.

❹ Its forward-angled legs are used while in flight to grasp its prey. As a dragonfly can fly swiftly or hover, and fly in any direction including sideways or backwards, it has a talent for hunting. It devours an enormous number of flying insects, including mosquitoes.

1 This text is an example of
- **A** an exposition.
- **B** a description.
- **C** an information report.

2 You would be likely to read this text in a book
- **A** of amazing facts.
- **B** about insects.
- **C** about inventions.

3 The fact that the dragonfly's eyes cover most of its head could be added to paragraph
- **A** two.
- **B** three.
- **C** four.

4 Which information has **not** been included in the text? Choose **two** answers.
- **A** Dragonflies have sharp jaws.
- **B** Dragonflies are ferocious predators.
- **C** Dragonflies are in danger of extinction.

5 A suitable caption for the photo would be
- **A** A dragonfly baby.
- **B** A dragonfly using legs to catch prey.
- **C** A dragonfly at rest.

6 Why might dragonflies be endangered?

....

....

....

....

....

....

7 Research how long dragonflies have been on earth.

Answers and explanations on page 115

Quokkas

1 Quokkas are Australian marsupials (a type of mammal that keeps its young in a pouch after birth) about the size of a cat. They are plant-eating animals that like to shelter in dense vegetation. The tunnels they make through this vegetation are used for feeding and as an escape route from predators.

2 Rottnest Island (near Perth), a fox-free island, is famous for its quokkas. It's also known for its good conservation practices. The happy nature of the quokkas makes them a popular tourist attraction. The island was named by a Dutch sea captain in 1696 who thought the animals were large rats that nested there in its vegetation! Quokkas are also found on Bald Island (near Albany) and in lower numbers in the south-west of Western Australia.

3 Their numbers have declined for numerous reasons including the introduction of dingoes and foxes, the spread of housing, logging, back-burning and large bushfires.

1. Which state of Australia is home to quokkas?
   - A Victoria
   - B South Australia
   - C Northern Territory
   - D Western Australia

2. The sea captain who named Rottnest Island was
   - A Australian.
   - B West Australian.
   - C Dutch.
   - D English.

3. Circle all the statements that are **not** true.
   - A Quokkas are bald.
   - B Humans are marsupials.
   - C Bushfires have reduced quokka numbers.
   - D Quokkas are large rats.

4. The information that quokkas are nocturnal animals could be added to
   - A paragraph one.
   - B paragraph two.
   - C paragraph three.
   - D the end of the text.

5. Why does Rottnest Island have more quokkas than the mainland? Choose **two** answers.
   - A It has been there since 1696.
   - B It has good conservation practices.
   - C It is fox free.
   - D It has lots of tourists.

6. Which animal is **not** closely related to the quokka?
   - A cat
   - B kangaroo
   - C wallaby
   - D possum

7. What kind of publication would include a text of this kind?

   ....

   ....

   ....

   ....

   ....

Answers and explanations on page 115

The spelling mistakes in these sentences have been underlined. Write the correct spelling on the lines.

1 Quokkas are smallish, firry animals.

....

2 Quokkas mostly feed during the nite-time.

....

3 They are frendly, sweet-natured animals.

....

4 The fox is a predattor of the quokka.

....

Read the text below. Choose the correct word or word group to complete the sentences.

Possums

The possum is a marsupial that lives ....(5).... trees and is mainly active at night. It ....(6).... a pointy face with ....(7).... pink nose, long, oval-shaped ears and a bushy tail. It is a shy animal ....(8).... it will eat nearly everything in your garden!

5 A through B over C under D in

6 A had B will have C has D is having

7 A a B an C the D some

8 A and B but C so D when

9 Which word is the noun in this sentence?

They make long, narrow tunnels.

A They B make C narrow D tunnels

10 Which word correctly completes the sentence?

They are nocturnal so they usually feed .... dusk and dawn.

A between B until C after D with

11 Choose the correct word to complete the sentence.

The mother keeps her babies in her pouch. .... has nipples there for feeding them.

A We B She C He D They

12 Which words tell **when**?

Last night some possums ran very quickly up the tree and across our roof.

A Last night
B very quickly
C up the tree
D across our roof

13 Which sentence is punctuated correctly?

A Its in the south-west of western Australia.
B It's in the south-west of western Australia.
C It's in the south-west of Western Australia.
D Its in the south-west of Western Australia.

14 Which sentence is punctuated **incorrectly**?

A The quokka, like the kangaroo and the wallaby, is a marsupial.
B Foxes, wild cats and dingoes prey on quokkas.
C Its hair is coarse, and brown or grey, in colour.
D Like the camel, quokkas can go for a long time without drinking.

Answers and explanations on pages 115–116

What should we change?

'Now we are settled outdoors, we can begin,' said Mr Kirkham.

'That's right, Year 3,' added Ms Blunt. 'The topic for today is: What would you like to change about our school?'

'I think our school day is far too long,' said Claudia.

'I agree,' said Mohammed. 'And homework should be abolished.'

'I disagree because we wouldn't get all our work done that way. Also, I wish we didn't have to wear free dress. I'd really prefer to wear a uniform,' said Beth in her bravest voice.

'No way,' Violet replied. 'They're always awful colours. Longer holidays would be good though.'

Seamus said, 'If we had our way we'd hardly come to school at all! We'd not learn anything. How about using the time a bit differently? Lessons in the morning and hobbies in the afternoon?'

'Marathon training and origami for me,' said Beth.

'I'd prefer robots and photography,' said Claudia. 'What do you think of our ideas, Ms Blunt?'

1. Where does the discussion take place?
   A in the Year 3 classroom **B** in the school hall **C** outdoors

2. Who announces the topic?
   A Claudia **B** Ms Blunt **C** Mr Kirkham

3. Most of the children say they would like
   A less time spent on lessons. **B** more time spent on lessons. **C** changes to the school rules.

4. Who gives a reason for their opinion? Choose **two** answers.
   A Beth **B** Claudia **C** Seamus

5. Who does **not** give a reason for their opinion?
   A Seamus **B** Mohammed **C** Violet

6. Would it be difficult for the teachers to accept Seamus's suggestion? Why or why not?

   ....

   ....

Answers and explanations on page 116

SPELLING

Rewrite the misspelt words in questions 1–4.

1 'Setle down, Year Three.'

2 You shouldnt behave like that!

3 I dislike those aweful, dull colours.

4 My favourite hobby is fotography.

5 Write three words from the word family that includes **learn**.

VOCABULARY

Circle the answers in questions 6–7 that have the nearest meaning to the underlined words.

6 Which outfit would you prefer?
- A rather
- B promote
- C adopt
- D love

7 Let's use our time differently.
- A separately
- B individually
- C otherwise
- D independently

8 Add a word from the text to the sentence.

Some students agree with me but others ………………… .

9 Write a word from the text to match the meaning.

put an end to …………………

Circle the word that does **not** belong.

10
- A alter
- B change
- C vary
- D preserve

11
- A hardly
- B nearly
- C rarely
- D seldom

GRAMMAR

12 Add a noun group from the text to the sentence.

In my view ………………… is far too long.

13 Which form of the verb completes the sentence correctly?

Don't you think that longer holidays ………………… better?
- A is
- B were
- C would be
- D are being

14 Write a prepositional phrase from the text that tells **how**.

Beth was shy but she spoke up ………………… .

15 Join the clauses with a conjunction.

We like our school ………………… the teachers listen to our opinions.
- A because
- B until
- C unless
- D while

PUNCTUATION

16 Circle the sentence that is punctuated correctly.
- A I agree, said Mohammed.
- B 'I agree,' said Mohammed.
- C 'I agree' said Mohammed.

Rewrite the sentences correctly.

17 thats right year 3 said ms blunt

18 whats your opinion mr kirkham asked seamus

Answers and explanations on page 116

What should we change?

'Now we are settled outdoors, we can begin,' said Mr Kirkham.

'That's right, Year 3,' added Ms Blunt. 'The topic for today is: What would you like to change about our school.?'

'I think our school day is far too long.' said Claudia.

'I agree,' said Mohammed. 'And homework should be abolished.'

'I disagree because we wouldn't get all our work done that way. Also, I wish we didn't have to wear free dress. I'd really prefer to wear a uniform,' said Beth in her bravest voice.

'No way,' Violet replied. 'They're always awful colours. Longer holidays would be good though.'

Seamus said, 'If we had our way we'd hardly come to school at all! We'd not learn anything. How about using the time a bit differently? Lessons in the morning and hobbies in the afternoon?'

'Marathon training and origami for me,' said Beth.

'I'd prefer robots and photography,' said Claudia. 'What do you think of our ideas, Ms Blunt?'

1. What type of text is this?
   - **A** an information report
   - **B** a discussion
   - **C** an exposition

2. How do the students respond to the question?
   - **A** with cheerful interest
   - **B** with annoyance
   - **C** with boredom

3. Which of these would help improve the students' comments?
   - **A** more interrupting of each other
   - **B** letting more students have a say
   - **C** giving more reasons to support their views

4. What does Violet mean when she says 'No way' (line 9)?
   - **A** I don't believe you.
   - **B** I can't believe anything you say.
   - **C** I would never choose to wear a uniform.

5. Which student is good at compromising (finding middle ground)?
   - **A** Beth
   - **B** Seamus
   - **C** Violet

6. How would you describe the school these children attend?
   - **A** strict and formal with many rules
   - **B** relaxed and informal with no rules
   - **C** casual and relaxed with some rules

7. Is there a change you would like to see at your school? Explain.

Answers and explanations on page 116

Casey's special memories

1. We used to live in a cul-de-sac. When you added up all the children in the houses it came to 17. There was always someone to play with and I didn't want to leave. Our new house was built on land at the back of my gran's house. I didn't find any friends for ages but it was fun having a sleepover at Gran's. Dad made me some wooden stilts and I stomped around the garden on them. They made me as tall as a giant.

2. On 13 September my Dad took me to hospital to see Scarlet, my newborn sister. I felt scared. She was tiny and soft and sort of crumpled. Her tiny fingers clutched one of my fingers. I soon decided I would always look after her very carefully. Mum gave me a present in a paper bag. It was a brand new, bouncy rubber ball that I still have.

1 What kind of street did Casey use to live in?

A a main road **B** a cul-de-sac **C** a through road

2 Where did Casey have a sleepover?

A at the hospital **B** at her new house **C** at her gran's house

3 Why didn't Casey want to move?

A She didn't think she'd like the new house.
B She would miss having so many playmates.
C She loved the garden where she lived.

4 How did Casey feel about her newborn sister?

A protective **B** jealous **C** excited

5 Why did Casey's mum give her a present?

A to make her feel special too
B to show her things had changed
C to make her practise her ball skills

6 What is Casey's attitude to change?

....

....

....

Answers and explanations on page 116

SPELLING

Rewrite the misspelt words in questions 1–4.

1 I have lots of special memmories.

2 Walking on woodden stilts is quite difficult.

3 I went to hosspittal to have my tonsils taken out.

4 Sometimes I feel scarred and a little bit frightened.

5 Write three words from the word family that includes **play**.

VOCABULARY

Circle the answers in questions 6–7 that have the nearest meaning to the underlined words.

6 Scarlet clutched my finger with her tiny fingers.
- A touched
- B linked
- C stroked
- D grasped

7 When she was born, Scarlet's skin was quite crumpled.
- A bent
- B crinkled
- C soft
- D unironed

8 Add a word from the text to the sentence.

I love my new, ... rubber ball.

9 Write a word from the text to match the meaning.

a street that is closed at one end

Circle the word that does **not** belong.

10
- A common
- B important
- C special
- D precious

11
- A scared
- B afraid
- C fearless
- D terrified

GRAMMAR

12 Add a noun group from the text to the sentence.

.... was built at the back of Gran's house.

13 Which form of the verb completes the sentence correctly?

It is fun .... a sleepover at Gran's.
- A had
- B having
- C having had
- D have

14 Write a prepositional phrase from the text that tells **how**.

Casey wanted to look after Scarlet ....

15 Join the clauses with a conjunction.
- A because
- B until
- C unless
- D while

It's hard to keep your balance .... walking on stilts.

PUNCTUATION

16 Circle the sentence that is punctuated correctly
- A Scarlet my newborn sister is very tiny.
- B Scarlet my new, born sister is very tiny.
- C Scarlet, my newborn sister, is very tiny.

Rewrite the sentences correctly.

17 on 13 september my sister was born

18 did you live in a cul de sac

Answers and explanations on pages 116–117

TEXTS IN CONTEXT

Casey's special memories

1. We used to live in a cul-de-sac. When you added up all the children in the houses it came to 17. There was always someone to play with and I didn't want to leave. Our new house was built on land at the back of my gran's house. I didn't find any friends for ages but it was fun having a sleepover at Gran's. Dad made me some wooden stilts and I stomped around the garden on them. They made me as tall as a giant.

2. On 13 September my Dad took me to hospital to see Scarlet, my newborn sister. I felt scared. She was tiny and soft and sort of crumpled. Her tiny fingers clutched one of my fingers. I soon decided I would always look after her very carefully. Mum gave me a present in a paper bag. It was a brand new, bouncy rubber ball that I still have.

1 In this text, Casey
- **A** reflects on events in her childhood.
- **B** recounts the events of her childhood.
- **C** explains why events happened in her childhood.

2 Where would this text **not** be found?
- **A** in a blog about memories
- **B** in a diary
- **C** in a note left on the fridge

3 The writing can best be described as
- **A** a rough draft of a story.
- **B** a public announcement.
- **C** personal thoughts.

4 The simile 'as tall as a giant' (line 6) suggests that Casey
- **A** likes using her stilts.
- **B** doesn't know whether or not she likes using her stilts.
- **C** doesn't like using her stilts.

5 The use of the first person (I, my, etc.) lets the reader
- **A** keep at a distance from Casey.
- **B** share Casey's thoughts and feelings.
- **C** learn about what others think of Casey.

6 How does the reader know that Casey has caring parents?
- **A** Casey says how they feel.
- **B** Casey describes how they behave.
- **C** Casey judges their actions.

Get creative

7 Write about one of your own childhood memories using Casey's text as a model.

Answers and explanations on page 117

READING AND COMPREHENSION

David Unaipon (1872–1967)

David Unaipon was a Ngarrindjeri man. He was born at the Point McLeay Christian Mission, south east of Adelaide, and showed great promise as a student there. When he left aged 13, he continued to teach himself about his favourite subjects.

David travelled around south-east Australia, often on foot, preaching Christianity. He gave lectures and was the first Indigenous Australian to have his writing published. His articles and booklets described the 'customs, beliefs and imaginings' of First Australians. He also represented First Nations people to the government and strongly influenced government policy in the 1920s and 1930s.

He was a passionate inventor. An improved set of shearer's scissors and a helicopter design based on the principle of the boomerang were examples (though he was never paid for these ideas). He tried to invent a machine that worked by using its own energy (perpetual motion) and he was still working on this project well into his nineties. His portrait is on Australia's 50-dollar note.

1 When was David born?

A 1872 **B** 1930 **C** 1967

2 Where is his portrait?

A in a gallery **B** at the mission **C** on a 50-dollar note

3 The Mission was set up to

A look after white preachers.
B care for First Australian people of the area.
C teach people how to invent things.

4 Why did First Australians want him as their spokesperson? Choose **two** answers.

A They respected him.
B They knew he had influence over government policy.
C He told them he would represent them.

5 Which skill did he **not** have?

A public speaking **B** making money from his inventions **C** writing

6 What makes David Unaipon special?

....

....

Answers and explanations on page 117

SPELLING

Rewrite the misspelt words in questions 1–4.

1 He conntinnued to teach himself.

2 Sometimes David traveled on foot.

3 His invenshion was based on how boomerangs fly.

4 The desine for his invention was interesting.

5 Write three words from the word family that includes **invent**.

VOCABULARY

Circle the answers in questions 6–7 that have the nearest meaning to the underlined words.

6 He wanted to make a perpetual motion machine.
- A activity
- B animation
- C movement
- D happening

7 You can see his portrait on the $50 note.
- A drawing
- B sketch
- C diagram
- D picture

8 Add a word from the text to the sentence.

Science was among his ____________ subjects.

9 Write a word from the text to match the meaning.

stood for or symbolised ____________

Circle the word that does **not** belong.

10
- A improved
- B tightened
- C corrected
- D bettered

11
- A kept
- B changed
- C shaped
- D influenced

GRAMMAR

12 Add a noun group from the text to the sentence.

____________ can be seen on a banknote.

13 Which form of the verb completes the sentence correctly?

David ____________ an inventor, an author and a preacher.
- A was
- B were
- C will be
- D being

14 Write a prepositional phrase from the text that tells **how**.

He travelled around the countryside ____________.

15 Join the clauses with a conjunction.

The government trusted David ____________ he was honest.
- A because
- B until
- C unless
- D while

PUNCTUATION

16 Circle the sentence that is punctuated correctly.
- A When he left he continued to study by himself?
- B When he left he continued to study by himself!
- C When he left, he continued to study by himself.

Rewrite the sentences correctly.

17 he travelled far and wide often on foot

18 david unaipon was a ngarrindjeri man

Answers and explanations on page 117

TEXTS IN CONTEXT

David Unaipon (1872–1967)

David Unaipon was a Ngarrindjeri man. He was born at the Point McLeay Christian Mission, south east of Adelaide, and showed great promise as a student there. When he left aged 13, he continued to teach himself about his favourite subjects.

David travelled around south-east Australia, often on foot, preaching Christianity. He gave lectures and was the first Indigenous Australian to have his writing published. His articles and booklets described the 'customs, beliefs and imaginings' of First Australians. He also represented First Nations people to the government and strongly influenced government policy in the 1920s and 1930s.

He was a passionate inventor. An improved set of shearer's scissors and a helicopter design based on the principle of the boomerang were examples (though he was never paid for these ideas). He tried to invent a machine that worked by using its own energy (perpetual motion) and he was still working on this project well into his nineties. His portrait is on Australia's 50-dollar note.

1. The purpose of this text is to
   - **A** inform the reader about a person's life story.
   - **B** persuade the reader to a cause.
   - **C** argue a point of view about a person.
2. The text can be labelled
   - **A** an autobiography.
   - **B** a biography.
   - **C** a scientific account.
3. Why are the words customs, beliefs and imaginings in speech marks?
   - **A** They are David's own words.
   - **B** They are words said by the author of the text.
   - **C** They are what the Mission wanted said.
4. The drawings beside David Unaipon's face on the $50 note are
   - **A** Indigenous symbols.
   - **B** information about who printed the note.
   - **C** sketches of some of his inventions.
5. The information that David received no payment (lines 13–14) is
   - **A** given a lot of emphasis.
   - **B** given no special emphasis.
   - **C** not worth mentioning.
6. What was David Unaipon's attitude to the relationship between First Australians and white people?

   ....

   ....

   ....

Get creative

7. Whose portrait would you like to see on an Australian banknote? Give three reasons.

Answers and explanations on page 117

Children on the First Fleet

Dear Diary

We've been studying the First Fleet at school. Today we learned about two of the youngest convicts on board.

Elizabeth Hayward was just 13 when the *Lady Penrhyn* set sail from Portsmouth to Australia with 101 female convicts. She'd stolen a gown, a bonnet and a bath cloak. Hey! I don't think the punishment fits the crime, do you?

John Hudson was only nine when he was sentenced to seven years transportation—and the judge wasn't certain he'd stolen anything! Here's the online transcript from his Old Bailey trial, dear Diary!

Court to Prisoner: *How old are you?*—John: *Going in nine.*
What business was you bred up in?—
John: *None, sometimes a chimney sweeper.*
Have you any father or mother?—John: *Dead.*
How long ago?—John: *I do not know.*

He was kept prisoner on an old hulk for three years before joining the convicts on the *Friendship*. It made me feel very upset.

See you
Mary

First Fleet: August 1787, Rio de Janeiro

1. What is the name of the youngest female convict?
   A Lady Penrhyn **B** Mary **C** Elizabeth Hayward

2. Where was John Hudson's trial held?
   A on an old hulk **B** on the *Friendship* **C** at the Old Bailey

3. Why doesn't the punishment fit the crime in Mary's view?
   A The sentence was far too harsh.
   B The sentence was just right.
   C The sentence was not harsh enough.

4. Choose **two** answers. The transcript reveals
   A how unfortunate John's life had been.
   B how cruel the interviewer was.
   C how pitiful John's case is.

5. Where did their ships stop during the journey?
   A Portsmouth **B** Rio de Janeiro **C** NSW

6. What made Mary so upset? 

Answers and explanations on pages 117–118

SPELLING

Rewrite the misspelt words in questions 1–4.

1 What have you been studdying?

2 She had stollen a bonnet.

3 A judje sentenced him to seven years.

4 He was kept a prisonier on an old hulk.

5 Write three words from the word family that includes **punishment**.

VOCABULARY

Circle the answers in questions 6–7 that have the nearest meaning to the underlined words..

6 Learning what happened made her very <u>upset</u>.
- A muddled
- B confused
- C distressed
- D unsettled

7 No-one was <u>certain</u> what had happened.
- A knowing
- B unsure
- C doubtful
- D sure

8 Add a word from the text to the sentence.

The .... should fit the crime.

9 Write a word from the text to match the meaning.

a written copy of something said

Circle the word that does **not** belong.

10
- A virtue
- B misconduct
- C crime
- D misdeed

11
- A condemned
- B pardoned
- C sentenced
- D convicted

GRAMMAR

12 Add a noun group from the text to the sentence.

.... transported convicts of all ages to Australia.

13 Which form of the verb completes the sentence correctly?

John Hudson .... only nine when he appeared in court.
- A was
- B were
- C will be
- D is being

14 Write a prepositional phrase from the text that tells **how**.

Mary was made to feel ....

15 Join the clauses with a conjunction.

He waited in a hulk .... it was time to sail to Australia.
- A because
- B until
- C unless
- D while

PUNCTUATION

16 Circle the sentence that is punctuated correctly.
- A Were there eleven ships in the First fleet?
- B Were there eleven ships in the First Fleet!
- C Were there eleven ships in the First Fleet?

Rewrite the sentences correctly

17 the *lady penrhyn* sailed from portsmouth

18 weve been learning about convicts

Answers and explanations on page 118

Children on the First Fleet

Dear Diary

We've been studying the First Fleet at school. Today we learned about two of the youngest convicts on board.

Elizabeth Hayward was just 13 when the *Lady Penrhyn* set sail from Portsmouth to Australia with 101 female convicts. She'd stolen a gown, a bonnet and a bath cloak. Hey! I don't think the punishment fits the crime, do you?

John Hudson was only nine when he was sentenced to seven years transportation—and the judge wasn't certain he'd stolen anything! Here's the online transcript from his Old Bailey trial, dear Diary!

Court to Prisoner: *How old are you?*—John: *Going in nine.*
What business was you bred up in?—
John: *None, sometimes a chimney sweeper.*
Have you any father or mother?—John: *Dead.*
How long ago?—John: *I do not know.*

He was kept prisoner on an old hulk for three years before joining the convicts on the *Friendship.* It made me feel very upset.

See you
Mary

First Fleet: August 1787, Rio de Janeiro

1 What is the purpose of this text?
   - **A** to persuade people to think kindly of convicts
   - **B** to explain why things happened
   - **C** to give details about a topic

2 How does Mary treat her diary?
   - **A** as someone she has recently met
   - **B** as someone she can confide in
   - **C** as something to do her homework in

3 Mary's diary entry includes
   - **A** an actual conversation from the 18th century.
   - **B** an imagined conversation from the 18th century.
   - **C** some conversation from an 18th-century play.

4 'See you' (line 17). What does Mary mean?
   - **A** hope to meet up again
   - **B** goodbye for now
   - **C** hope to see you around

5 Choose **all** that apply. The First Fleet stamp
   - **A** emphasises the success of the journey.
   - **B** exaggerates the suffering of the convicts.
   - **C** ignores the convicts.

6 Can Mary's information be trusted? 

7 Work with a partner. Play the roles of Elizabeth and John. Imagine you meet each other in Sydney Cove. Have a conversation about your past.

Answers and explanations on page 118

READING AND COMPREHENSION

The Second First Fleet

About a decade before Australia's Bicentenary, Jonathan King had the idea of building a replica of the First Fleet—the eleven ships that had sailed to Australia in 1788, bringing convicts to the colony.

King thought the re-enactment of that nine-month-long voyage would be a memorable way to celebrate the colony's birthday. Not everyone, including the government, fully agreed with him and he found it difficult to get funding for his project.

Eventually it won some famous backers. The Queen of England, Thor Heyerdahl (who crossed the Pacific Ocean on a raft) and Sir Edmund Hillary (who was first to reach the peak of Mt Everest) made it possible through their support for King to continue with his plans.

There were numerous setbacks along the way. However, on Australia Day in 1988, eleven square-rigged ships sailed through the heads to be welcomed by around 3000 vessels in Sydney Harbour.

1 How many ships were there in the First Fleet?

A eleven **B** nine **C** seven

2 Why is Sir Edmund Hillary famous?

A He crossed the Pacific in a raft.
B He was first to climb Mt Everest.
C He built a replica of the First Fleet.

3 Which of these would **not** have been a setback to the re-enactment?

A The funding dried up when the ships reached Rio de Janeiro.
B Some ships were damaged and others withdrew.
C Two ships arrived at the last minute to bring their number to eleven.

4 Why was the government against King's idea? Choose **two** answers.

A It thought no-one would attend.
B It didn't want to offend Indigenous Australian people.
C It didn't want to draw attention to Australia's convict past.

5 Why would Heyerdahl and Hillary have supported King's idea?

A They were both clever. **B** They were both adventurers. **C** They both wanted the publicity.

6 Why might Queen Elizabeth have supported King's project? ....

....

Answers and explanations on page 118

SPELLING

Rewrite the misspelt words in questions 1–4.

1 Australia's Bicenteenery was held in 1988.

2 He hoped it would be a memmorable voyage.

3 The goverment was not in favour of the plan.

4 Numorous setbacks spoilt their journey.

5 Write three words from the word family that includes **sailed**.

VOCABULARY

Circle the answers in questions 6–7 that have the nearest meaning to the underlined words.

6 He wanted to build a <u>replica</u> fleet.

A miniature B photocopy
C similar D duplicate

7 They had <u>numerous</u> setbacks.

A endless B many
C various D several

8 Add a word from the text to the sentence.

Some .... people offered their support for the plan.

9 Write a word from the text to match the meaning.

worth remembering; unforgettable

Circle the word that does **not** belong.

10 A celebrate B honour
C remember D publicise

11 A support B help
C supply D aid

GRAMMAR

12 Add a noun group from the text to the sentence.

was Jonathan King's idea.

13 Which form of the verb completes the sentence correctly?

He .... the idea of building a replica of the First Fleet.

A has B had
C was having D having had

14 Write a prepositional phrase from the text that tells **how**.

They made it possible to continue ....

15 Join the clauses with a conjunction.

The re-enactment couldn't begin .... they had funding.

A because B until
C unless D while

PUNCTUATION

16 Circle the sentence that is punctuated correctly.

A The Bicentenary celebrated the colony's birthday.
B The bicentenary celebrated the colonys birthday.
C The Bicentenary celebrated the Colonys Birthday.

Rewrite the sentences correctly.

17 he crossed the pacific ocean on a raft

18 there were 3000 vessels in sydney harbour

Answers and explanations on page 118

TEXTS IN CONTEXT

The Second First Fleet

About a decade before Australia's Bicentenary, Jonathan King had the idea of building a replica of the First Fleet—the eleven ships that had sailed to Australia in 1788, bringing convicts to the colony.

King thought the re-enactment of that nine-month-long voyage would be a memorable way to celebrate the colony's birthday. Not everyone, including the government, fully agreed with him and he found it difficult to get funding for his project.

Eventually it won some famous backers. The Queen of England, Thor Heyerdahl (who crossed the Pacific Ocean on a raft) and Sir Edmund Hillary (who was first to reach the peak of Mt Everest) made it possible through their support for King to continue with his plans.

There were numerous setbacks along the way. However, on Australia Day in 1988, eleven square-rigged ships sailed through the heads to be welcomed by around 3000 vessels in Sydney Harbour.

1. What is the main purpose of this text?
   - **A** to discuss
   - **B** to inform
   - **C** to describe

2. Where would you **not** find this text?
   - **A** in a Wikipedia article
   - **B** in a reference book
   - **C** on talkback radio

3. The facts are presented
   - **A** roughly in the order they happened.
   - **B** as a series of comparisons.
   - **C** as a series of comments.

4. The brackets are used to
   - **A** provide an explanation.
   - **B** add emphasis.
   - **C** express feelings.

5. What is the author's point of view about the re-enactment?
   - **A** supportive
   - **B** unbiased
   - **C** disapproving

6. Was King's project a complete success?

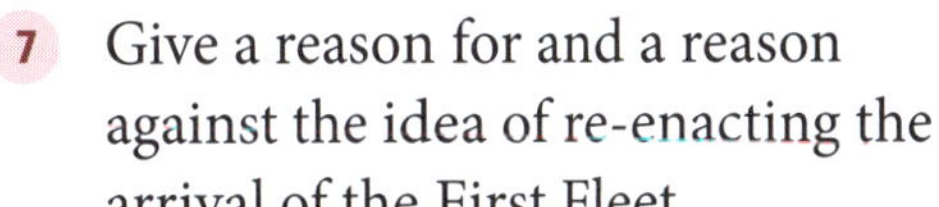

7. Give a reason for and a reason against the idea of re-enacting the arrival of the First Fleet.

Answers and explanations on pages 118–119

Fun with magnets

Experiment 1

You'll need: glass jar, plasticine, paper clips, table, magnet

Method: Make a 6 cm–long snake from plasticine. Add dots for eyes so it looks realistic.

Hold two paper clips together, on top of each other. Press them hard into the back of the snake.

Place the snake in the jar so the paper clips are near the glass wall.

Hold the magnet against the jar and move it up and down. Your snake should move too!

Experiment 2

You'll need: plasticine, pencil with eraser, horseshoe magnet

Method: Make a cone shape out of the plasticine. Smooth the flat, round bottom so it sits well on the table.

Press the eraser end of the pencil into the point of the cone until it stands vertically without tipping.

Balance the magnet on the pencil tip. The horseshoe magnet should slowly swing to a north–south direction.

Results: ....

1. How many experiments are there?
   - **A** one
   - **B** two
   - **C** three

2. How do you make the plasticine snake look realistic?
   - **A** Make it very long.
   - **B** Make it very thin.
   - **C** Add dots for eyes.

3. Why does the jar for Experiment 1 need to be made of glass?
   - **A** so it can be sterilised
   - **B** so you can see through it
   - **C** so it won't break

4. Choose **two** answers. Plasticine is used because
   - **A** it is soft and pliable.
   - **B** children often use it.
   - **C** it holds its shape.

5. Why do you need a horseshoe-shaped magnet for Experiment 2?
   - **A** Horseshoes bring good luck.
   - **B** It needs to stick to the pencil tip.
   - **C** It needs to balance on the pencil tip.

6. Do you think the title suits the text?

....

....

Answers and explanations on page 119

SPELLING

Rewrite the misspelt words in questions 1–4.

1 You need to make a snake out of plastiseen.

....

2 Have you done any experriments in science at school? ....

3 The pencil should be standing verticaly. ....

4 I couldn't find a pencil with an erazer.

....

5 Write three words from the word family that includes **magnet**.

....

....

VOCABULARY

Circle the answers in questions 6–7 that have the nearest meaning to the underlined words.

6 Hold the paper clips carefully.
A clutch B clench
C grip D carry

7 You must smooth the base of the plasticine so it sits flat.
A level B polish
C iron D press

8 Add a word from the text to the sentence.
The wizard's hat was shaped like a ....

9 Write a word from the text to match the meaning.
perpendicular to the horizon; straight up

....

Circle the word that does **not** belong.

10 A unalike B convincing
C realistic D lifelike

11 A anything B something
C nothing D everything

GRAMMAR

12 Add a noun group from the text to the sentence.

....
is balanced on the tip of the pencil.

13 Which form of the verb completes the sentence correctly?
Were you .... fun when doing these experiments?
A have B having
C had D have had

14 Write a prepositional phrase from the text that tells **how**.
The pencil must stand ....
....

15 Join the clauses with a conjunction.
What were you doing .... I was doing these experiments?
A because B until
C unless D while

PUNCTUATION

16 Circle the sentence that is punctuated correctly.
A Did it turn in a North–South Direction?
B Did it turn in a north–south direction!
C Did it turn in a north–south direction?

Rewrite the sentences correctly.

17 she already had a glass jar paper clips and a magnet

....

....

18 youll need some plasticine for this experiment

....

....

Answers and explanations on page 119

Fun with magnets

Experiment 1

You'll need: glass jar, plasticine, paper clips, table, magnet

Method: Make a 6 cm–long snake from plasticine. Add dots for eyes so it looks realistic.

Hold two paper clips together, on top of each other. Press them hard into the back of the snake.

Place the snake in the jar so the paper clips are near the glass wall.

Hold the magnet against the jar and move it up and down. Your snake should move too!

Experiment 2

You'll need: plasticine, pencil with eraser, horseshoe magnet

Method: Make a cone shape out of the plasticine. Smooth the flat, round bottom so it sits well on the table.

Press the eraser end of the pencil into the point of the cone until it stands vertically without tipping.

Balance the magnet on the pencil tip. The horseshoe magnet should slowly swing to a north–south direction.

Results: ....

1. The purpose of this text is to
   - **A** provide some factual information.
   - **B** recall events in a sequence.
   - **C** tell you how to do something.

2. Where might you find this text?
   - **A** in an educational book
   - **B** in a book of games
   - **C** in a book of rules

3. The structure of this text is similar to that of a
   - **A** book review.
   - **B** game show.
   - **C** recipe.

4. Why are there commands at the beginning of most sentences?
   - **A** to show who is in charge
   - **B** to provide a set of instructions to follow
   - **C** to turn the experiments into a game

5. The author hasn't filled in the 'Results:' because they
   - **A** don't know what the results are.
   - **B** mean to fill in this section later.
   - **C** have already recorded the results.

6. In what way is the picture connected to the text? Explain.

....

....

....

....

....

7. Do one of the experiments. What did you learn about magnets? Explain.

Answers and explanations on page 119

Androcles and the Lion

Androcles hated being a slave. One day, taking his chances, he escaped into the forest. As he wandered about looking for food, he came across a Lion groaning with pain.

The Lion looked up beseechingly at Androcles and held out his bleeding, swollen paw. Trembling with fear, Androcles pulled out the large thorn stuck there. The Lion was enormously grateful. He licked the hands and face of his new friend.

Unfortunately, not long after, both were captured. The Emperor sentenced Androcles to be thrown to the lions. The Court watched with enjoyment as a caged animal was released into the arena. He rushed towards Androcles, roaring and baring his teeth.

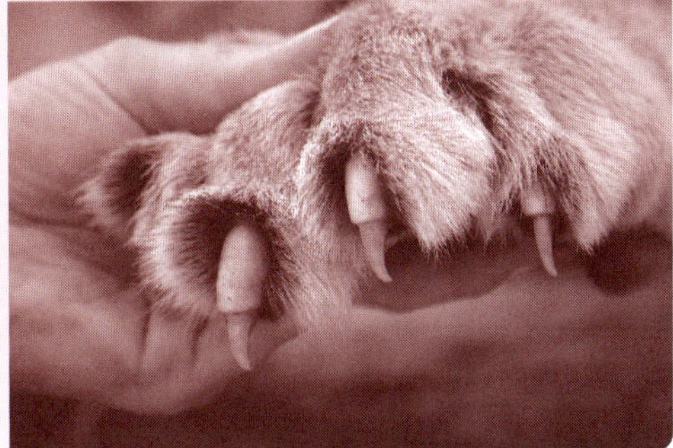

To everyone's surprise, the Lion suddenly skidded to a halt. He began to lick Androcles's hands and face in a most affectionate way.

When the Emperor heard Androcles's story, he pardoned him and the Lion was set free to live in his native forest.

(Adapted from an Aesop's fable.)

1 What was Androcles?

A a Lion **B** an Emperor **C** a slave

2 Where did he escape to?

A the Court **B** the forest **C** the arena

3 Why did Androcles tremble with fear (line 5)?

A He thought the thorn might be poisonous.
B He thought the Lion might kill him.
C He planned to capture the Lion.

4 How did the Lion feel after the thorn was removed? Choose **two** answers.

A extremely hungry
B grateful to Androcles
C affectionate towards his new friend

5 Why was Androcles sentenced to be eaten by lions?

A as a punishment for his escape **B** as a punishment for the Lion **C** to annoy the crowd

6 Why did the Emperor pardon Androcles and the Lion? ....

....

....

....

Answers and explanations on page 119

SPELLING

Rewrite the misspelt words in questions 1–4.

1 The Lion was groneing with pain.

....

2 His paw was swowllen and bleeding.

....

3 Unfourtunately, they were captured.

....

4 The Lion was bearing his teeth.

....

5 Write three words from the word family that includes **large**.

....

....

VOCABULARY

Circle the answers in questions 6–7 that have the nearest meaning to the underlined words.

6 Androcles was trembling with fear.
- A wobbling
- B throbbing
- C fluttering
- D shaking

7 To the Emperor's surprise, the Lion looked fondly at the slave.
- A disappointment
- B horror
- C amazement
- D alarm

8 Add a word from the text to the sentence.

The thorn had made his paw .... and bloody.

9 Write a word from the text to match the meaning.

pleadingly ....

Circle the word that does **not** belong.

10
- A unfortunately
- B sadly
- C regrettably
- D luckily

11
- A displeasure
- B satisfaction
- C amusement
- D enjoyment

GRAMMAR

12 Add a noun group from the text to the sentence.

It licked .... affectionately.

13 Which form of the verb completes the sentence correctly?

Both Androcles and the Lion .... captured a few days later.
- A are being
- B was
- C were
- D were being

14 Write a prepositional phrase from the text that tells **how**.

The Court watched ....

15 Join the clauses with a conjunction.

The Emperor was surprised .... he'd thought the Lion would eat Androcles.
- A because
- B until
- C unless
- D while

PUNCTUATION

16 Circle the sentence that is punctuated correctly.
- A The Lion licked Androcles hands and face.
- B The Lion licked Androcles's hands and face.
- C The lion licked Androcles's hands and face.

Rewrite the sentences correctly.

17 he held out his bleeding swollen paw

....

....

18 when he heard the story he forgave them

....

....

Answers and explanations on pages 119–120

Androcles and the Lion

Androcles hated being a slave. One day, taking his chances, he escaped into the forest. As he wandered about looking for food, he came across a Lion groaning with pain.

The Lion looked up beseechingly at Androcles and held out his bleeding, swollen paw. Trembling with fear, Androcles pulled out the large thorn stuck there. The Lion was enormously grateful. He licked the hands and face of his new friend.

Unfortunately, not long after, both were captured. The Emperor sentenced Androcles to be thrown to the lions. The Court watched with enjoyment as a caged animal was released into the arena. He rushed towards Androcles, roaring and baring his teeth.

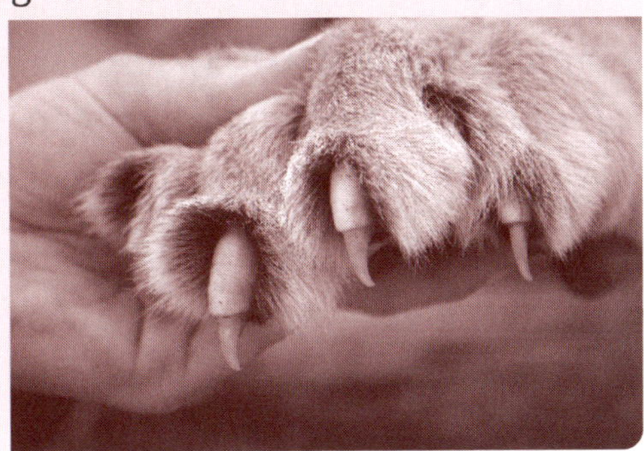

To everyone's surprise, the Lion suddenly skidded to a halt. He began to lick Androcles's hands and face in a most affectionate way.

When the Emperor heard Androcles's story, he pardoned him and the Lion was set free to live in his native forest.

(Adapted from an Aesop's fable.)

1 The purpose of this text is to
- **A** present opinions.
- **B** entertain and instruct.
- **C** show how something is done.

2 The narrator shows more admiration for
- **A** the Emperor than the Lion.
- **B** Androcles than the Lion.
- **C** the Lion than the Emperor.

3 Which action leads to the climax of the story?
- **A** Androcles escapes from his master.
- **B** Androcles pulls the thorn from the Lion's paw.
- **C** The Emperor has Androcles thrown to the lions.

4 Why does the word Lion always have a capital letter in the text?
- **A** It is normal to capitalise animals' names.
- **B** It was Aesop's custom to capitalise all his words.
- **C** It shows the Lion is a character in the story.

5 Which statement is **not** a message of the text?
- **A** You can't trust anyone in this world.
- **B** Be kind to animals.
- **C** Gratitude is an important virtue.

6 Who is the main character: Androcles or the Lion? Explain.

....

....

....

....

Get creative

7 Read 'The Lion and the Mouse', another Aesop's fable. Write a sentence that sums up its moral.

Answers and explanations on page 120

Lost (an extract)

'It's no good,'' Gretel said. 'We're lost, Hansel. I can't see the breadcrumbs you dropped. The trail has disappeared. I think the birds must have eaten them.'

'You're right,'' Hansel replied. 'Why ever do our parents keep losing us in the forest? It isn't fair!'

'It's dark,' Gretel said in despair. 'We'll never get home now. We'll have to spend another night starving under a pile of leaves with only the moonlight for company.'

'The moon. That's it, Gretel. It's a crescent moon. Just what we need. I remember learning how to find north from a crescent moon. You draw an imaginary line connecting the horns of the moon and extend it down to the horizon. When you look towards that point you will face north.'

'You're a genius, bro. I'd say we should head off that way. Do you agree?'

'Yup. Stay close, sis. Fingers crossed. Let's go.'

1. Where are Hansel and Gretel?
   - **A** on the moon
   - **B** in the forest
   - **C** at home
2. Who dropped the breadcrumbs?
   - **A** Hansel
   - **B** Gretel
   - **C** the parents
3. What causes Gretel's despair?
   - **A** fear of the dark
   - **B** dislike of moonlight
   - **C** dread of not getting home
4. Why does Gretel think they'll go hungry? Choose **two** answers.
   - **A** She doesn't like berries.
   - **B** They've run out of food.
   - **C** They have no way of getting more food.
5. Why does Gretel call Hansel a genius?
   - **A** His clever idea might save them.
   - **B** She's heard people say he is.
   - **C** She isn't clever herself.
6. How good is Hansel at solving problems?

....

....

Answers and explanations on page 120

SPELLING

Rewrite the misspelt words in questions 1–4.

1 The birds ate all the bredcrums.

....

2 For a moment she felt full of dispear.

....

3 I like the slim shape of a cresent moon.

....

4 You need to draw an imaginairy line.

....

5 Write three words from the word family that includes **dark**.

....

VOCABULARY

Circle the answers in questions 6–7 that have the nearest meaning to the underlined words.

6 I remember a trick for learning how to find north.

A recognise B recall
C summon D know

7 The breadcrumbs had disappeared.

A withdrawn B retreated
C faded D gone

8 Add a word from the text to the sentence.

She was frightened and full of ....

9 Write a word from the text to match the meaning.

a shape resembling a segment of a ring tapering to points at the ends

....

Circle the word that does **not** belong.

10 A factual B actual
C imaginary D real

11 A lengthen B abbreviate
C extend D expand

GRAMMAR

12 Complete the noun group with an adjective from the text.

Did you see the .... moon in the night sky?

13 Which form of the verb completes the sentence correctly?

You .... north if you turn towards those trees.

A have faced B will face
C had faced D faces

14 Write a prepositional phrase from the text that tells **how**.

'I'm frightened and it is getting dark,' Gretel said ....

15 Join the clauses with a conjunction.

If we go north .... we'll reach our home.

A as well as B then
C therefore D but

PUNCTUATION

16 Circle the sentence that is punctuated correctly.

A 'Well never get home now.'
B 'We'll never get home now.
C 'We'll never get home now."

Rewrite the sentences correctly.

17 youre a genius bro Gretel said

....

....

18 youre right Hansel replied

....

....

Answers and explanations on page 120

Lost (an extract)

'It's no good,'' Gretel said. 'We're lost, Hansel. I can't see the breadcrumbs you dropped. The trail has disappeared. I think the birds must have eaten them.'

'You're right,'' Hansel replied. 'Why ever do our parents keep losing us in the forest? It isn't fair!'

'It's dark,' Gretel said in despair. 'We'll never get home now. We'll have to spend another night starving under a pile of leaves with only the moonlight for company.'

'The moon. That's it, Gretel. It's a crescent moon. Just what we need. I remember learning how to find north from a crescent moon. You draw an imaginary line connecting the horns of the moon and extend it down to the horizon. When you look towards that point you will face north.'

'You're a genius, bro. I'd say we should head off that way. Do you agree?'

'Yup. Stay close, sis. Fingers crossed. Let's go.'

1 This extract is from a
- **A** recount.
- **B** narrative.
- **C** discussion.

2 Does the reader know why the children are in the forest?
- **A** No. We aren't told why their parents left them there.
- **B** Yes. We can guess that the parents want their children to be survivors.
- **C** Yes. We can guess that the parents want to get rid of their children.

3 The extract comes from the .... of the text 'Lost'.
- **A** beginning
- **B** middle
- **C** ending

4 Which statement is true? This text contains
- **A** the author's point of view.
- **B** the parents' point of view.
- **C** the children's points of view.

5 'Fingers crossed' (line 15) is
- **A** a joke about crossing your fingers.
- **B** an idiom meaning let's hope for good luck.
- **C** an expression meaning link your fingers in mine.

6 Could Gretel be described as a drama queen?

....

....

....

....

....

7 Write an ending for the text.

Answers and explanations on page 120

First flight

To: floandjo@bigland.com

Hi Auntie Flo

Guess what! I flew in an aeroplane all by myself. We flew from my home in Perth to Hanoi in Vietnam. There were other people on the plane, such as the pilot and other passengers of course, but I didn't have any of my family with me.

The flight attendant took a picture of me in my seat. I had a window seat. Looking out at the clouds was amazing. I wanted to jump out of the window and bounce up and down on their fluffy white softness. You weren't allowed do that though, so I stayed in my seat with my seatbelt fastened.

I was flying to Hanoi to stay with my big sister for the school holidays. She lives there with her baby son, Binh. We visited a temple at Hoan Kiem Lake and went to the Dong Xuan night markets. Now I am back home and I can't wait to fly there again.

Love

Duy

1 Duy flew from Perth to

- **A** Hoan Kiem Lake.
- **B** Binh.
- **C** Hanoi.
- **D** Dong Xuan.

2 Where is Duy when he is writing this email?

- **A** at home
- **B** with his sister
- **C** on the plane
- **D** in Vietnam

3 Why wasn't Duy allowed to bounce on the clouds? Choose **two** answers.

- **A** It is impossible to get out of a plane window.
- **B** His mother had told him not to.
- **C** He had his seatbelt on.
- **D** Leaving a plane in flight is forbidden.

4 The exclamation mark after 'Guess what!' suggests Duy's

- **A** fear.
- **B** excitement.
- **C** amusement.
- **D** shock.

5 What kind of relationship does Duy have with his aunt? Choose **two** answers.

- **A** close
- **B** distant
- **C** friendly
- **D** difficult

6 What is Duy most keen to tell his auntie?

- **A** that he met Binh
- **B** that he flew to Vietnam by himself
- **C** that he didn't jump on the clouds
- **D** that he had a window seat

7 Why can't Duy wait to return to Vietnam?

....

....

....

....

....

Answers and explanations on pages 120–121

The spelling mistakes in these sentences have been underlined. Write the correct spelling on the lines.

1 The <u>propellar</u> on the aircraft was already spinning

....

2 There was an <u>enawmouse</u> carpark at the airport.

....

3 I could see the whole <u>environmeant</u> set out below me.

....

4 An airport is an <u>extreamly</u> busy place.

....

Read the text below. Choose the correct word or word group to complete the sentences.

The Pilot

Hi Uncle Jo

I ....(5).... my first flight as a pilot today. Our landing was a bit bumpy but I blamed the westerly wind. ....(6).... everything ....(7).... very well, thank goodness. I hear you ....(8).... on a flight of mine next week. I look forward to that.

Best wishes

Sammy

5 **A** has **B** had **C** have **D** having

6 **A** Otherwise **B** Because **C** Always **D** When

7 **A** was **A** goed **C** went **D** were

8 **A** am **B** were **C** was **D** will be

9 Which word is the noun in this sentence?

I looked out of the small glass window.

A looked **B** small **C** glass **D** window

10 Which word correctly completes the sentence?

The aeroplane flew higher and higher .... it was way above the clouds.

A because **B** until **C** for **D** but

11 Choose the correct word to complete the sentence.

My sister made spring rolls for our lunch. .... is such a good cook!

A We **B** She **C** He **D** They

12 Which words tell **when**?

We were able to arrive at the airport at lunchtime.

A were able **B** to arrive **C** at the airport **D** at lunchtime

13 Which sentence is punctuated correctly?

A They were served an orange a salad roll and a glass of milk.

B They were served an orange, a salad roll and a glass of milk.

C They were served an orange a salad roll and a glass of milk!

D They were served an orange, a salad roll, and a glass of milk.

14 Which sentence is punctuated **incorrectly**?

A The flight attendant said, 'Fasten your seatbelts, please.'

B She asked him to fasten his seatbelt.

C 'May I unfasten my seatbelt now, please?' asked Duy?

D At take-off time, everyone fastened their seatbelts.

Answers and explanations on page 121

READING AND COMPREHENSION

The superb lyrebird

The superb lyrebird is native to Australia and lives in forests to the west of the Great Dividing Range. Fossils held in the Australian Museum show lyrebirds lived in Australia as far back as 15 million years ago.

Superb lyrebirds have strong legs with long toes and claws. Their wings are small and not strongly muscled. They are famous mimics. They don't only copy sounds made by other birds and animals—they often imitate sounds made by a train, a chainsaw, a car engine or even a mobile phone!

Courtship offers another chance for the male to sing. He mounts the display mound he has built, raises his long, colourful tail feathers in a spectacular show above his head and 'sings' for about twenty minutes to his smaller, less showy mate.

1. A superb lyrebird's toes are
   A long. **B** short. **C** medium sized.

2. Superb lyrebirds live .... of the Great Dividing Range.
   A south **B** east **C** west

3. They are known as ground-dwelling birds because
   A they fly down to the ground.
   B they spend much more time at ground level than in the air.
   C the male builds mounds on the ground.

4. Choose **two** answers. The female superb lyrebird
   A doesn't sing during courtship.
   B has stronger wings than the male's.
   C is a good mimic.

5. Which information is **not** in the text?
   A Fossils of lyrebirds from long ago are held in the Australian Museum.
   B Another species of lyrebird is the Albert's lyrebird.
   C The male superb lyrebird puts on a striking courtship display.

6. What is most surprising about the lyrebird's ability to imitate?

   ....

   ....

Answers and explanations on page 121

SPELLING

Rewrite the misspelt words in questions 1–4.

1 I have seen fosils of lyrebirds

....

2 They are in the Australian Musuem.

....

3 Their wings are not strongly mussled.

....

4 Look at its collorfull tail!

....

5 Write three words from the word family that includes **built**.

....

VOCABULARY

Circle the answers in questions 6–7 that have the nearest meaning to the underlined words.

6 The male lyrebird mounts his mound and sings his song.

A raises B climbs
C grows D raises

7 His tail is spectacular and attracts interest.

A eye-catching B intense
C clashing D glassy

8 Add a word from the text to the sentence.

Lyrebirds are .... for their mimicry.

9 Write a word from the text to match the meaning.

remains of plants or animals from long ago, preserved as rock

....

Circle the word that does **not** belong.

10 A imitates B sings
C mimics D copies

11 A strong B powerful
C large D muscular

GRAMMAR

12 Complete the noun group with an adjective from the text.

When courting, the .... lyrebird displays his tail.

13 Which relating (having) verb or verb group completes the sentence correctly?

Lyrebirds .... small wings and sharp claws.

A had B have
C have had D are having

14 Complete the sentence with a prepositional phrase that tells **where**.

Lyrebirds live ....

....

15 Join the clauses with a conjunction.

The male lyrebird, ... the female, is a good mimic.

A as well as B then
C therefore D but

PUNCTUATION

16 Circle the sentence that is punctuated correctly.

A The male shows off to the smaller, less showy female.
B The male shows off to the smaller less showy female!
C The male shows off to the smaller, less showy female!

Rewrite the sentences correctly.

17 they dont only copy sounds made by birds

....

....

18 they can even imitate a mobile phone

....

....

Answers and explanations on page 121

TEXTS IN CONTEXT

The superb lyrebird

❶ The superb lyrebird is native to Australia and lives in forests to the west of the Great Dividing Range. Fossils held in the Australian Museum show lyrebirds lived in Australia as far back as 15 million years ago.

❷ Superb lyrebirds have strong legs with long toes and claws. Their wings are small and not strongly muscled. They are famous mimics. They don't only copy sounds made by other birds and animals—they often imitate sounds made by a train, a chainsaw, a car engine or even a mobile phone!

❸ Courtship offers another chance for the male to sing. He mounts the display mound he has built, raises his long, colourful tail feathers in a spectacular show above his head and 'sings' for about twenty minutes to his smaller, less showy mate.

1. The purpose of this text is to
   - **A** praise the beauty of the lyrebird.
   - **B** give information about the lyrebird.
   - **C** explain where you can find lyrebirds.

2. Where would you be likely to find this text?
   - **A** in an email
   - **B** in a text message
   - **C** in Wikipedia
   - **D** in a newspaper

3. The word superb tells you
   - **A** the species of lyrebird being described.
   - **B** how attractive the lyrebird is.
   - **C** what a beautiful tail the lyrebird has.

4. The exclamation mark at the end of paragraph 2 expresses surprise that
   - **A** the lyrebird can imitate sounds.
   - **B** a bird can be so up to date with its imitations.
   - **C** anything would want to imitate other animals.

5. The picture is a useful addition to the text because it
   - **A** shows the shape and size of the male's tail.
   - **B** is in black and white.
   - **C** shows many important details of the bird's habitat.

6. Find a picture of a lyre, an ancient Greek musical instrument. Why do you think the lyrebird was named after this instrument?

   ....

   ....

Get creative

7. Find a recording of the superb lyrebird imitating sounds. For example, the BBC's clip of David Attenborough's Bird Sounds from the Lyrebird on the internet. Now practise and record your own imitation of a sound you hear in your environment.

Answers and explanations on page 121

The moon

The moon is a roundish object in space. At night it looks like a light in the sky. In fact, the light we see comes from the sun shining on its surface.

There are dead volcanoes, craters and lava flows on the moon's hard, rocky surface. Some craters were caused a long time ago by rocky objects (meteoroids and asteroids) crashing into it. Below this there are further layers of rock and a core of metal. Some frozen water has been detected at the poles. At night temperatures reach minus 173 °C.

The moon circles the earth every four weeks. It doesn't change shape although it looks as if it does. There's a time during each month when the moon isn't visible at all and another when you can see just a thin slither in the shape of a crescent (called the new moon).

Since men in space suits reached the moon in 1969, we've begun to learn much more about it.

1 What shines on the moon's surface?

A volcanoes　**B** lava　**C** the sun

2 What shape is the new moon?

A roundish　**B** a star　**C** a crescent

3 Which statement is true?

A The moon often changes its shape.
B There is some ice on the moon.
C The moon has a smooth surface.

4 Which statements are false? Choose **two** answers.

A The moon is made of cheese.
B There is plenty of water on the moon.
C The moon does not give out light.

5 Why can't humans live on the moon? Choose **all** that apply.

A There isn't enough water.　**B** There isn't enough food.　**C** It's far too cold.

6 Why will our knowledge about the moon continue to change?

....

....

Answers and explanations on page 121

SPELLING

Rewrite the misspelt words in questions 1–4.

1 Do you know what corsed those craters?

2 The moon has three main laiers.

3 An asteroyd is a rocky object.

4 The moon is sometimes cresent shaped.

5 Write three words from the word family that includes **night**.

VOCABULARY

Circle the answers in questions 6–7 that have the nearest meaning to the underlined words.

6 The moon has a rocky <u>surface</u>.
A outer layer
B outline
C shape
D appearance

7 There are times when the moon isn't <u>visible</u>.
A hidden
B clear
C detectable
D remarkable

8 Add a word from the text to the sentence.

The water on the poles of the moon is ______.

9 Write a word from the text to match the meaning.

openings at the top of a volcano or round holes in the ground made by a meteor

Circle the word that does **not** belong.

10 A inside
B core
C surface
D middle

11 A round
B ball-shaped
C circular
D arched

GRAMMAR

12 Complete the noun group with an adjective from the text.

There are ______ layers of rock beneath the moon's surface.

13 Which relating (being) verb completes the sentence correctly?

We ______ begun to learn more about the moon since 1969.

A had
B having
C have
D has

14 Complete the sentence with a prepositional phrase that tells **when**.

The moon looks like a light in the sky ______.

15 Join the clauses with a conjunction.

The moon is unsuitable for humans ______ I don't want to live there.

A as well as
B then
C so
D but

PUNCTUATION

16 Circle the sentence that is punctuated correctly.
A There's a time when the moon isn't visible.
B Theres a time when the moon isn't visible.
C There's a time when the moon isnt visible!

Rewrite the sentences correctly.

17 rocky objects meteoroids and asteroids caused the craters

18 we learned about the moon and its qualities

Answers and explanations on page 122

The moon

The moon is a roundish object in space. At night it looks like a light in the sky. In fact, the light we see comes from the sun shining on its surface.

There are dead volcanoes, craters and lava flows on the moon's hard, rocky surface. Some craters were caused a long time ago by rocky objects (meteoroids and asteroids) crashing into it. Below this there are further layers of rock and a core of metal. Some frozen water has been detected at the poles. At night temperatures reach minus 173 °C.

The moon circles the earth every four weeks. It doesn't change shape although it looks as if it does. There's a time during each month when the moon isn't visible at all and another when you can see just a thin slither in the shape of a crescent (called the new moon).

Since men in space suits reached the moon in 1969, we've begun to learn much more about it.

1 The purpose of this text is to
- **A** prepare people for living on the moon.
- **B** disprove myths about the moon.
- **C** inform people about the nature of the moon.

2 Where might this text be found?
- **A** in a book of experiments
- **B** in a book about space
- **C** in a book about survival

3 The text is made up mainly of
- **A** facts.
- **B** fiction.
- **C** opinions.

4 The topic of the text makes it necessary to
- **A** make poetic comparisons.
- **B** include technical terms.
- **C** arouse strong feelings.

5 Which is **not** a subject of the text?
- **A** the moon's gravity
- **B** what the moon is made of
- **C** what we see when we look at the moon

6 Is the illustration a photograph? Why or why not?

....

....

....

....

....

....

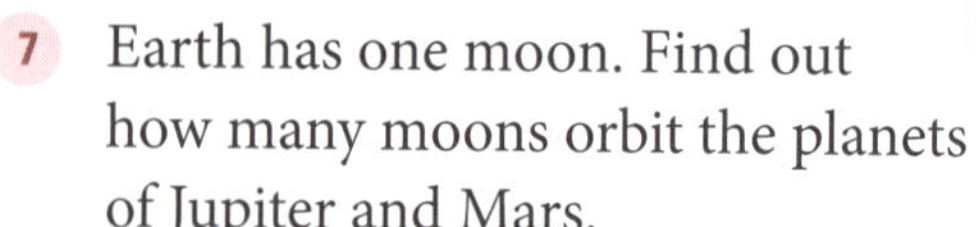

7 Earth has one moon. Find out how many moons orbit the planets of Jupiter and Mars.

Answers and explanations on page 122

READING AND COMPREHENSION

Who am I?

My body is unusual—
without a bone or limb.
I have no teeth. I have no eyes.
I'm both a her and him!

You might think me a baldy.
In fact, you would be wrong.
There's hairs on all my segments, and
I'm muscly, slim and strong.

Anterior to posterior
I'm a very handsome chap.
Cut off my tail, I'll not complain.
I rarely fuss or flap.

I'll simply grow a new tail,
get on quickly with my work.
I'll shift the soil. I'll help it breathe,
recycle all your murk.

The truth is I'm a hero
so why do people squirm?
It's time I got a medal.
I'm a prize-deserving worm!

1 How does the worm describe its body?

A handsome **B** bald **C** unusual

2 What does the worm have on all its segments?

A murk **B** hairs **C** muscles

3 Which statement is a matter of opinion?

A I'm a very handsome chap. **B** I'm muscly, slim and strong. **C** I have no teeth.

4 Which statements about the worm are **not** true? Choose **two** answers.

A It has both male and female parts.
B It is a vertebrate.
C It is useless.

5 What can worms do that most living creatures can't?

A Turn themselves inside out.
B Grow hair on their bodies.
C Regrow a part of their bodies.

6 Does the worm deserve a medal? Why or why not?

....

....

Answers and explanations on page 122

SPELLING

Rewrite the misspelt words in questions 1–4.

1 Each segmeant of a worm has muscles.

....

2 He thinks he's hansome!

....

3 Why do you complane about everything?

....

4 Do you sqirm when you see a worm?

....

5 Write three words from the word family that includes **new**.

....

....

VOCABULARY

Circle the answers in questions 6–7 that have the nearest meaning to the underlined words.

6 Is it unusual to be without bones, teeth and eyes?

A curious B incredible
C special D odd

7 You have nothing to complain about!

A consent B protest
C attack D disagree

8 Add a word from the text to the sentence.

You can .... your food waste using worms.

9 Write a word from the text to match the meaning.

behind or at the rear of; bottom

....

Circle the word that does **not** belong.

10 A hassle B fret
C soothe D fuss

11 A shrink B grow
C sprout D develop

GRAMMAR

12 Complete the noun group with an adjective from the text.

The worm grew a .... tail.

13 Which relating (being) verb or verb group completes the sentence correctly?

The truth .... I think I deserve a medal.

A was B is
C are D will be

14 Complete the sentence with an adverb that tells **how**.

Worms like to wriggle .... through the soil.

15 Join the clauses with a conjunction.

I want a worm farm .... my mum says I can't have one.

A as well as B then
C therefore D but

PUNCTUATION

16 Circle the sentence that is punctuated correctly.

A I'm muscly, slim and strong.
B Im muscly, slim and strong.
C I'm muscly slim and strong.

Rewrite the sentences correctly.

17 its time I got a medal

....

....

18 im a prize deserving worm

....

....

Answers and explanations on page 122

TEXTS IN CONTEXT

Who am I?

❶ My body is unusual—
without a bone or limb.
I have no teeth. I have no eyes.
I'm both a her and him!

❷ You might think me a baldy.
In fact, you would be wrong.
There's hairs on all my segments, and
I'm muscly, slim and strong.

❸ Anterior to posterior
I'm a very handsome chap.
Cut off my tail, I'll not complain.
I rarely fuss or flap.

❹ I'll simply grow a new tail,
get on quickly with my work.
I'll shift the soil. I'll help it breathe,
recycle all your murk.

❺ The truth is I'm a hero
so why do people squirm?
It's time I got a medal.
I'm a prize-deserving worm!

1 The purpose of this poem is to
- A express feelings and reflections.
- B tell a story.
- C recount experiences.

2 Choose **all** that apply. The poem is amusing because it
- A gives a worm a human voice.
- B includes rhymes that make you smile.
- C is full of riddles.

3 The worm supports its conclusion with a series of
- A events.
- B reasons.
- C random facts.

4 An important feature of this poem is its
- A use of repetition.
- B brisk, lively rhythm.
- C use of imagery.

5 What kind of 'person' is the worm?
- A modest and shy
- B bitter and complaining
- C confident and proud

6 What is the message of the poem? Explain.

Get creative

7 Write another stanza to go between stanzas four and five.

Answers and explanations on page 122

Buy our B-MADE honey

- Our honey—B-MADE Honey—is the best honey money can buy. Only available from your local chemist or farmers' markets.
- Yes, honey lasts forever. You won't ever have to worry about the use-by date of our B-MADE honey.
- It makes a delicious food. What about lemon and honey chicken for dinner? Or put it on pancakes for breakfast? In your tea or as a dip with lemon and yoghurt? Honey contains vitamins and minerals and is way better for you than sugar.
- But there's more. You can use it to heal wounds, soothe burns and cure sore throats. Its healing properties as a natural bandage have been written about since ancient times. Hospitals around the world now use commercially made, honey-infused bandages. Honey is magical!
- So don't delay. Add B-MADE honey to your shopping list today. B-MADE honey, made from the nectar of flowers by bees, just so YOU can blossom.

1 Where can B-MADE honey be bought?

A at supermarkets or chemists **B** at local shops or markets
C at local chemists or farmers' markets

2 How long does honey last?

A a long time **B** forever **C** until its use-by date

3 The claim in the text that honey is healthier than sugar is

A backed up with evidence. **B** not backed up with evidence. **C** proved beyond a doubt.

4 Choose **two** answers. Honey is described as

A good to eat when mixed with other foods.
B good to lift your spirits.
C having world-famous healing properties.

5 The flowers in the photograph are to

A show honey is from the natural world. **B** add some decoration. **C** attract bees.

6 Is the choice of the word 'magical' (line 16) a fair description of honey? ....

....

....

....

Answers and explanations on pages 122–123

SPELLING

Rewrite the misspelt words in questions 1–4.

1 The local kemist sells our honey.

2 Lemon and honey with chicken is delishious.

3 Is that brand commersially available?

4 Honey dates back to ainshent times.

5 Write three words from the word family that includes **use**.

VOCABULARY

Circle the answers in questions 6–7 that have the nearest meaning to the underlined words.

6 Honey lasts forever.
- A for all time
- B for a long time
- C till you're blue in the face
- D repeatedly

7 The honey healed the sore on my knee.
- A saved
- B solved
- C cured
- D mended

8 Add a word from the text to the sentence.

Did you know honey .... minerals?

9 Write a word from the text to match the meaning.

a sweet liquid produced by plants and made into honey by bees ....

Circle the word that does **not** belong.

10
- A ancient
- B current
- C earliest
- D olden

11
- A blossom
- B flower
- C bloom
- D fade

GRAMMAR

12 Complete the noun group with an adjective from the text.

My jar of honey doesn't have a .... date.

13 Which auxiliary (helping) verb completes the sentence correctly?

B-Made honey .... sure to be good for you.
- A was
- B were
- C is
- D are

14 Complete the sentence with a prepositional phrase that tells **where**.

You can put honey .... instead of sugar.

15 Join the clauses with a conjunction.

Honey contains vitamins .... it must be good for you.
- A as well as
- B then
- C so
- D but

PUNCTUATION

16 Circle the sentence that is punctuated correctly.
- A Our honey's sold at farmers' markets.
- B Our honey's sold at farmer's markets.
- C Our honeys sold at farmers' markets.

Rewrite the sentences correctly.

17 honey is magical

18 does honey have a use by date

Answers and explanations on page 123

Buy our B-MADE honey

- Our honey—B-MADE Honey—is the best honey money can buy. Only available from your local chemist or farmers' markets.
- Yes, honey lasts forever. You won't ever have to worry about the use-by date of our B-MADE honey.
- It makes a delicious food. What about lemon and honey chicken for dinner? Or put it on pancakes for breakfast? In your tea or as a dip with lemon and yoghurt? Honey contains vitamins and minerals and is way better for you than sugar.
- But there's more. You can use it to heal wounds, soothe burns and cure sore throats. Its healing properties as a natural bandage have been written about since ancient times. Hospitals around the world now use commercially made, honey infused bandages. Honey is magical!
- So don't delay. Add B-MADE honey to your shopping list today. B-MADE honey, made from the nectar of flowers by bees, just so YOU can blossom.

1 The purpose of the text is to persuade people to
- **A** appreciate the work of bees.
- **B** buy B-MADE honey.
- **C** eat more honey of any brand.

2 The audience targeted by this text is
- **A** children who don't like sugar.
- **B** health-conscious adults who want a quality product.
- **C** people looking for a bargain that will last a long time.

3 The text is organised as a series of
- **A** claims and promises.
- **B** facts and stories.
- **C** jokes and recipes.

4 The B in the name of the honey ('B-MADE')
- **A** is a pun on the word bee.
- **B** refers to its Vitamin B content.
- **C** stands for the word Best.

5 Why is the word 'YOU' (line 18) in capital letters?

....

....

6 What methods of persuasion are used in the text?

....

....

7 Create a short advertisement for another product that uses **two** of the techniques used in 'Buy our B-MADE honey'.

Answers and explanations on page 123

Traditional dress

Most countries have a traditional form of dress. Two well-known examples are the sari from India and the kimono from Japan.

The sari, worn mainly by women, dates back to at least 3000 BCE. It is made from a single length of fabric (the word means strip of cloth in Sanskrit) and is draped gracefully around the body. It can be made from cotton or more luxurious silk. Choices of colours and patterns carry meanings related to beliefs, status and geographical areas.

The kimono (the word means clothing in Japanese) has been worn since the 9th century. Today it is worn mainly for special occasions such as tea ceremonies or weddings. A kimono is made from material cut in straight lines and sewn together. It has long, wide sleeves and is worn belted with a wide sash (obi). The middle section hangs to the ankle. Its colours and images symbolise the seasons and good fortune.

1 A traditional form of dress is worn in

A two countries. **B** most countries. **C** some countries.

2 An obi is

A a wide sash. **B** a kimono. **C** a sari.

3 What is Sanskrit?

A a way of dressmaking **B** a country **C** a language

4 When would silk saris be worn? Choose **two** answers.

A at grand ceremonies **B** at weddings **C** for everyday activities

5 In what way is a kimono different from a sari?

A Its colours have meanings.
B The material is cut and sewn.
C It is worn on special occasions.

6 Why do people wear traditional dress?

....

....

Answers and explanations on page 123

SPELLING

Rewrite the misspelt words in questions 1–4.

1 I will make a sari from this lenth of fabric.

....

2 I will wear it drapped around my body.

....

3 This kimono is made from lucsurious silk.

....

4 I only wear this dress on special ocasions.

....

5 Write three words from the word family that includes **made**.

....

....

VOCABULARY

Circle the answers in questions 6–7 that have the nearest meaning to the underlined words.

6 My sari is made from the most <u>luxurious</u> silk.

A plain B soft
C splendid D pampered

7 The kimono and sari are <u>well known</u> around the world.

A recognised B celebrated
C common D complicated

8 Add a word from the text to the sentence.

Her .... was that of a married woman.

9 Write a word from the text to match the meaning.

has been handed down over time

....

Circle the word that does **not** belong.

10 A chiefly B only
C mainly D mostly

11 A fabric B cloth
C material D silk

GRAMMAR

12 Complete the noun group with an adjective from the text.

The kimono is worn at .... ceremonies.

13 Which auxiliary (helping) verb or verb group completes the sentence correctly?

The kimono .... worn since the 9th century.

A is being B will be
C has been D have been

14 Complete the sentence with a prepositional phrase that tells **when**.

The sari dates back to ....

15 Join the clauses with a conjunction.

I have a kimono .... I don't know how to put it on yet.

A as well as B then
C so D but

PUNCTUATION

16 Circle the sentence that is punctuated correctly.

A Its worn with an obi a wide sash around the waist.
B (It's worn with an obi a wide sash) around the waist.
C It's worn with an obi (a wide sash) around the waist.

Rewrite the sentences correctly.

17 it has long wide sleeves

....

....

18 i like its colours pattern and design

....

....

Answers and explanations on page 123

TEXTS IN CONTEXT

Traditional dress

Most countries have a traditional form of dress. Two well-known examples are the sari from India and the kimono from Japan.

The sari, worn mainly by women, dates back to at least 3000 BCE. It is made from a single length of fabric (the word means strip of cloth in Sanskrit) and is draped gracefully around the body. It can be made from cotton or more luxurious silk. Choices of colours and patterns carry meanings related to beliefs, status and geographical areas.

The kimono (the word means clothing in Japanese) has been worn since the 9th century. Today it is worn mainly for special occasions such as tea ceremonies or weddings. A kimono is made from material cut in straight lines and sewn together. It has long, wide sleeves and is worn belted with a wide sash (obi). The middle section hangs to the ankle. Its colours and images symbolise the seasons and good fortune.

1. The purpose of the text is to
   A express thoughts and feelings.
   B recount past events.
   C present factual information.

2. Where might you find this text?
   A in an advertising brochure
   B in a book about the history of dress
   C in a biography

3. Which answer summarises the structure of the kimono text?
   A how it's made, its appearance, its history
   B its history, how it's made, its appearance
   C its appearance, how it's made, its history

4. How does the reference chain for the word sari affect the text? Choose **two** answers.
   A It links information about the topic.
   B It makes the writing livelier.
   C It avoids repeating the topic word.

5. The kimono in the picture doesn't have a sash because
   A it is on display and not being worn.
   B most kimonos don't have sashes.
   C it is from the 9th century.

6. What is traditional about a sari and a kimono?

....

....

....

....

Get creative

7. Draw a picture to show what Australians traditionally wear outdoors in summer.

Answers and explanations on pages 123–124

Do cats make better pets than dogs?

Alfie: Absolutely! You don't have to take them for walks when it's really hot.

Di: I disagree. Walks keep you fit and give you exercise. That's a plus for dogs.

Margaret: Yes. And dogs are more intelligent than cats. My dog 'talks' to me.

Charles: No way. It's cats who are the intelligent ones.

Alfie: True. They're smart *and* they look after themselves.

Margaret: I admit our puppy is very demanding. He always wants my attention. Then I have to teach him to use the litter, feed him, check for fleas and bath him. But he's worth it. He's the most friendly, comforting, loyal pet you could have.

Charles: When our cat was a playful kitten she caused chaos. But now she's no trouble and most days she curls up close to me. Intelligent *and* cuddly! Cats win in my view.

Margaret: Cats? Cuddly? You must be dreaming!

1. Who checks her puppy for fleas?
   A Alfie **B** Di **C** Margaret

2. Who speaks only once?
   A Di **B** Alfie **C** Charles

3. What do Alfie's reasons for his opinion tell you about him?
   A He's probably lazy. **B** He's allergic to dogs. **C** He's very caring.

4. What do Margaret's comments tell you about her? Choose **two** answers.
   A She is shy.
   B She has a forceful personality.
   C She has a caring nature.

5. Margaret's comment 'You must be dreaming!' (line 14)
   A shows she agrees with Charles.
   B makes fun of Charles's comment.
   C restates her earlier opinions.

6. Whose arguments are the most convincing? Why?

....

....

Answers and explanations on page 124

SPELLING

Rewrite the misspelt words in questions 1–4.

1 I dissagree with what you say.

....

2 Cats can look after themsleves.

....

3 My cat is friendly, inteligent and comforting.

....

4 Kittens can cause kaos!

....

5 Write three words from the word family that includes **attention**.

....

....

VOCABULARY

Circle the answers in questions 6–7 that have the nearest meaning to the underlined words.

6 My dog is smart and intelligent.

A imaginative B clever
C knowledgeable D well informed

7 Do you agree you were wrong about cats being cuddly?

A decide B permit
C admit D suggest

8 Add a word from the text to the sentence.

My baby sister is always wanting Mum's ....

9 Write a word from the text to match the meaning.

a state of confusion and disorder ....

Circle the word that does **not** belong.

10 A loyal B faithful
C helpful D devoted

11 A minus B bonus
C benefit D plus

GRAMMAR

12 Complete the noun group with an adjective from the text.

Our old cat was once a .... kitten.

13 Which auxiliary (helping) verb or verb group completes the sentence correctly?

When our cat .... born, her eyes were blue.

A were B is
C was D will be

14 Complete the sentence with a prepositional phrase that tells **when**.

My cat curls up close to me

....

15 Join the clauses with a conjunction.

She liked cats .... dogs.

A as well as B then
C therefore D but

PUNCTUATION

16 Circle the sentence that is punctuated correctly.

A I feed, check for fleas and bath my dog.
B I feed, check for fleas, and bath my dog.
C I feed check for fleas and bath my dog.

Rewrite the sentences correctly.

17 thats my opinion

....

....

18 theyre such loyal friendly animals

....

....

Answers and explanations on page 124

TEXTS IN CONTEXT

Do cats make better pets than dogs?

Alfie: Absolutely! You don't have to take them for walks when it's really hot.

Di: I disagree. Walks keep you fit and give you exercise. That's a plus for dogs.

Margaret: Yes. And dogs are more intelligent than cats. My dog 'talks' to me.

Charles: No way. It's cats who are the intelligent ones.

Alfie: True. They're smart *and* they look after themselves.

Margaret: I admit our puppy is very demanding. He always wants my attention. Then I have to teach him to use the litter, feed him, check for fleas and bath him. But he's worth it. He's the most friendly, comforting, loyal pet you could have.

Charles: When our cat was a playful kitten she caused chaos. But now she's no trouble and most days she curls up close to me. Intelligent *and* cuddly! Cats win in my view.

Margaret: Cats? Cuddly? You must be dreaming!

1 This text is
- **A** an explanation.
- **B** a discussion.
- **C** a description.

2 Where would you be most likely to come across this text?
- **A** in a book about pets
- **B** on the radio
- **C** in the newspaper?

3 The text is made up of a series of
- **A** unconnected statements.
- **B** responses to other's comments.
- **C** claims without reasons.

4 The topic of the text is stated in the
- **A** opening line.
- **B** second line.
- **C** title.

5 Why does Margaret say 'My dog 'talks' to me' (line 4)?
- **A** She believes it is true.
- **B** She is lying to win the argument.
- **C** She is exaggerating to make people laugh.

6 Write a caption for the photo that links it to the text.

....

....

7 Interview three people about their opinion of the topic. Write down the most convincing comment you received.

Answers and explanations on page 124

READING AND COMPREHENSION

The Little Refugee (by Anh Do and Suzanne Do, illustrated by Bruce Whatley)

What I like about the picture book, *The Little Refugee*, is that it is a true story. I always like reading stories about real people. The story is narrated by Anh Do. He tells it in a way that makes it feel as if he is talking just to me.

His Vietnamese family, who fought with the Australian and Americans in a war in their country, find their lives are in danger. As they try to escape with others in a crowded boat, they face storms and thieving pirates. Eventually, they make it to Australia where they find a whole new set of problems to overcome. However, they do well and Anh Do makes his parents proud.

I admire the way Anh Do stays so hopeful and cheerful even though things are very grim and frightening. I was also pleased to learn that the profits from selling the book go to a charity that looks after poor and disabled children in Vietnam. Anh Do is my new hero!

Brad (aged 9)

1. Who is *The Little Refugee* written by?
   A Brad   **B** Anh Do and Suzanne Do   **C** Suzanne Do

2. Who narrates the story?
   A Brad   **B** Anh Do   **C** Suzanne Do

3. Why did Anh Do want to leave Vietnam?
   A He wanted to try living in a new place.
   B He had lost his family.
   C He and his family were in danger.

4. Why was the boat so crowded? Choose **two** answers.
   A Many people were trying to escape.
   B The owner thought the more, the merrier.
   C Not enough boats were available.

5. Why does Brad admire Anh Do?
   A He goes on a crowded boat.
   B He gives the profits of his book to help needy people.
   C He is his hero.

6. What might the 'new set of problems' (line 9) include? ....

....

Answers and explanations on page 124

SPELLING

Rewrite the misspelt words in questions 1–4.

1 Anh Do belongs to a Veetnameze family.

2 Theeving pirates attacked their ship.

3 Evenchually they reached Australia.

4 The prophets were given to charity.

5 Write three words from the word family that includes **danger**.

VOCABULARY

Circle the answers in questions 6–7 that have the nearest meaning to the underlined words.

6 Their lives were in <u>danger</u>.
A trouble B emergency
C peril D hot water

7 <u>Eventually</u>, they reached Australia.
A In conclusion B Afterwards
C Later D Finally

8 Add a word from the text to the sentence.
Their new problems were also difficult to ....

9 Write a word from the text to match the meaning.
a person looked up to because of their bravery or good character ....

Circle the word that does **not** belong.

10 A unhappy B pessimistic
C hopeful D sad

11 A gloomy B bleak
C grim D encouraging

GRAMMAR

12 Complete the noun group with an adjective from the text.
The Little Refugee is a .... story.

13 Which verb or verb group completes the sentence correctly?
Anh Do .... born in Vietnam.
A is B was
C will be D must be

14 Complete the sentence with a prepositional phrase that tells **how**.
They tried to escape ....

15 Join the clauses with a conjunction.
Anh Do came to Australia .... learned to speak English.
A as well as B then
C therefore D but

PUNCTUATION

16 Circle the sentence that is punctuated correctly.
A His family who fought, in the war was in danger.
B His family, who fought in the war, was in danger.
C His family, who fought in the war was in danger.

Rewrite the sentences correctly.

17 an dho is my new hero

18 the books profits were given to a charity

Answers and explanations on pages 124–125

TEXTS IN CONTEXT

The Little Refugee (by Anh Do and Suzanne Do, illustrated by Bruce Whatley)

❶ What I like about the picture book, *The Little Refugee*, is that it is a true story. I always like reading stories about real people. The story is narrated by Anh Do. He tells it in a way that makes it feel as if he is talking just to me.

❷ His Vietnamese family, who fought with the Australian and Americans in a war in their country, find their lives are in danger. As they try to escape with others in a crowded boat, they face storms and thieving pirates. Eventually, they make it to Australia where they find a whole new set of problems to overcome. However, they do well and Anh Do makes his parents proud.

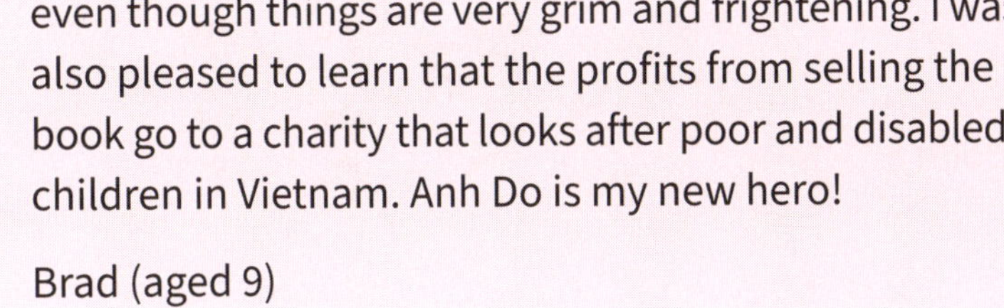

❸ I admire the way Anh Do stays so hopeful and cheerful even though things are very grim and frightening. I was also pleased to learn that the profits from selling the book go to a charity that looks after poor and disabled children in Vietnam. Anh Do is my new hero!

Brad (aged 9)

1. What is this text?
   - **A** an advertisement
   - **B** an information report
   - **C** a book review
2. Who would be likely to find this text helpful? Choose **all** that apply.
   - **A** children
   - **B** adults
   - **C** librarians
3. Which paragraph does **not** contain Brad's opinions?
   - **A** paragraph one
   - **B** paragraph two
   - **C** paragraph three
4. *The Little Refugee* is
   - **A** a story based on fact.
   - **B** a story based on fiction.
   - **C** fantasy.
5. What makes Brad feel close to Anh Do?
   - **A** his friendly, personal way of telling his story
   - **B** the fact that he is Vietnamese
   - **C** the fact that his story is about adventures
6. How is the photo related to the text?

....

....

....

....

....

Get creative

7. Find out three things that happened to Anh Do as an adult living in Australia.

Answers and explanations on page 125

The Fitters

Who are we? We are a group of trainers who can help you get fit and stay that way.

What do we offer? We give personal attention to your every need. Want to run a marathon? We can help. Want to make the football team at school? No problems. Want to be able to touch your toes? Trust us.

What does it cost? We offer a low weekly fee that everyone can afford.

What do our clients say about us?

I like The Fitters. They do what they promise. I was as fit as a fiddle after only one month of training. And I made the football team! (Ally, 10 years old)

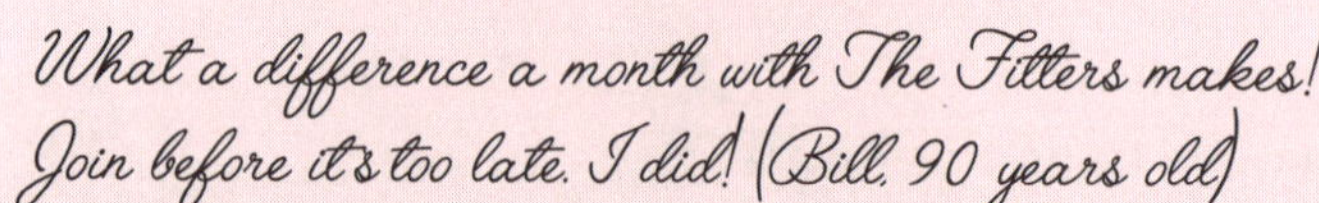

What are you waiting for? Join The Fitters and you won't look back. Join today and receive the added bonus of our special autumn reduction.

1. When are payments made to The Fitters?
   - **A** daily
   - **B** weekly
   - **C** monthly
   - **D** annually

2. In which season is the offer of a bonus made?
   - **A** spring
   - **B** summer
   - **C** autumn
   - **D** winter

3. What is the purpose of this text?
   - **A** to encourage young and old to be active
   - **B** to persuade people to join The Fitters
   - **C** to admire people who are healthy
   - **D** to persuade people to enjoy their lives more

4. Where might you find this text? Choose **all** that apply.
   - **A** in an encyclopedia
   - **B** in a magazine
   - **C** on a website
   - **D** in a newspaper

5. The comments are in handwriting to suggest that
   - **A** real people wrote these comments.
   - **B** young and old are happy at The Fitters.
   - **C** The Fitters are very popular.
   - **D** Bill has old-fashioned handwriting.

6. Ally's comment (lines 8–10) is **not** very convincing because
   - **A** girls don't play football.
   - **B** she's only 10 and wouldn't have an opinion.
   - **C** she's only a girl.
   - **D** she could have achieved what she did without The Fitters.

7. Do you think this is an effective advertisement? Why or why not?

   ....

   ....

   ....

   ....

   ....

   ....

   ....

Answers and explanations on page 125

There is one spelling mistake in each sentence. Write the correct spelling of each word.

1 Do you get enough excersize?

....

2 I found my excess weight dissapeared very quickly.

....

3 Evenchually I made the football team.

....

4 I joined the group in Febuary.

....

Read the text below. Choose the correct word to complete the sentences.

Yoga for children

Have you ...(5)... of introducing your children to yoga? It will make them more ...(6)... and peaceful. It will build their strength and muscle tone. A course of yoga would make ...(7)... healthy gift for any child. Order a course now ...(8)... it is too late.

5 A thinked B thought C thinking D thunk

6 A calm B calmer C calmest D calmly

7 A an B a C the D one

8 A until B after C when D before

9 Which word is the noun in this sentence?

I decided to take up yoga immediately.

A decided B take C yoga D immediately

10 Which word or word group correctly completes the sentence?

I have some new sports socks .... a new sports bag.

A because B but C therefore D as well as

11 Choose the correct word to complete the sentence.

Mum does yoga and now .... am doing it too.

A I B you C it D they

12 Which words tell **how**?

I went running through the mud to the oval and arrived just in time.

A went running B through the mud C to the oval D just in time

13 Which sentence is punctuated correctly?

A Mary asked 'Can I come to the tennis please."

B Mary asked 'Can I come to the tennis please?"

C Mary asked, 'Can I come to the tennis please."

D Mary asked, 'Can I come to the tennis, please?"

14 Which punctuation shows Noriko is excited to be starting yoga lessons?

A 'I'm starting yoga tomorrrow,' cried Noriko.

B 'I'm starting yoga tomorrrow?' cried Noriko.

C 'I'm starting yoga tomorrrow!' cried Noriko.

D 'I'm starting yoga tomorrrow.' cried Noriko.

Answers and explanations on page 125

ANSWERS

Unit 1A PAGE 8

1. **B**. See line 6.
2. **B**. See line 2.
3. **A** and **C**. You can work out that no-one likes to be sick but not everyone likes school.
4. **A** and **B**. You can work out that some people don't like computers or wearing woollies but everyone disapproves of bullies.
5. **A**. You can work out that the poet states what her likes and dislikes are with confidence and without hesitation.
6. Responses will vary. You can judge almost any of the poet's likes or dislikes are unexpected. It will depend on your own experiences and what you think is a usual or common attitude.

Unit 1B PAGE 9

1. measles
2. wearing
3. favourite
4. chocolate
5. Suggested answers: surprises, surprised, surprising, unsurprised
6. A.
7. C.
8. Bullies
9. fan
10. C.
11. B.
12. pies
13. C.
14. to bed
15. She
16. I don't like cold winter mornings.
17. Did you get a surprise?
18. I'm off to bed now.

Unit 1C PAGE 10

1. **B**. The poet tells the reader her views about what she likes and dislikes as well as what she likes best.
2. **A**. The question breaks the listing of the poet's opinions and brings the reader into the poem.
3. **A**. The writer knows contrast will make the poem better. Too much of the same thing can become monotonous.
4. **C**. The poem itself doesn't offer any proof of whether the poet is a boy or a girl but the picture is of a girl with her gran.
5. **B**. The apostrophe indicates some letters have been omitted from the word. It is short for the word 'because'.
6. Responses will vary. Your point of view may depend on whether you share some of the same opinions as the poet, whether you like the voice you hear speaking to you from the poem or whether you think she has the qualities you like in a friend.
7. Your poem should express your own opinions about the things you like and dislike. As you are using the text as a model you should write in verses where the second and last line rhyme.

Unit 2A PAGE 11

1. **B**. See line 2.
2. **A**. See line 8.
3. **C**. You can work out that the flattened sides of its muscular tail would help it move easily through water.
4. **A** and **C**. You can work out that, with its nostrils out of the water, it can breathe air while the rest of its body can remain hidden.
5. **B**. You can work out that a strong set of teeth in working order is needed in order to attack and eat large animals.
6. You can judge that the most likely cause of so few crocodiles surviving would be their many predators such as turtles, birds, reptiles and other crocodiles.

Unit 2B PAGE 12

1. crocodiles
2. tropical
3. nostrils
4. survive
5. Suggested answers: build, builds, building, builder
6. C.
7. A.
8. inhabit
9. wetlands
10. C.
11. B.
12. eggs/crocodiles
13. A.
14. in salt water
15. she
16. They visit rivers, streams and wetlands.
17. They eat wild pigs, cattle, buffaloes and humans.
18. When the eggs are ready to hatch, the babies chirp.

Unit 2C PAGE 13

1. **C**. The text provides information about the saltwater crocodile's habitat, its physical form, its eating habits and its young.
2. **B**. Information about the world's largest living reptile is likely to be found in a book about reptiles.
3. **A**. This new information is connected to the crocodile's food catch, a subject touched on in paragraph two.
4. **A**. Australians are well known for abbreviating words and adding a 'y' or 'ie' ending, as with the word salties.
5. **B**. The writer presents known facts about salties in a straightforward way.
6. Responses will vary. People need to be educated about the dangers of crocodiles (i.e. become crocwise). Salties submerge themselves underwater and may not be expected or noticed in waters where humans choose to swim. Tourists especially need to be warned as they may be unaware of the dangers.
7. Any three of the following: Freshwater crocodiles are usually smaller, have narrower snouts, have more evenly sized teeth, are more unlikely to attack humans and breed in the tropical dry season rather than the wet season.

Unit 3A PAGE 14

1. **C**. See lines 5, 7 and 11.
2. **B**. See line 5.
3. **A**. You can work out that disobeying a rule could get them and their dog into trouble with the law.
4. **A** and **C**. Will is not in charge of the bed and how Tom moves in his sleep is out of his control anyway.
5. **B**. You can work out that there is evidence that Tom and Alisa look after Will properly: they won't let him disobey the rules and they take him for walks.
6. Responses may vary. You can judge that Will's owners would think his letter was cheeky and uncalled for! On the other hand, they might find it amusing.

Unit 3B PAGE 15

1. quite
2. answer
3. grateful
4. whimper
5. Suggested answers: understands, understood, understanding, misunderstand
6. **A**.
7. **C**.
8. improve
9. disturbs
10. **A**.
11. **D**.
12. bedclothes
13. **C**.
14. into the butcher's shop
15. they
16. Don't let your dogs inside our gate!
17. Will you visit the butcher's shop?
18. I'd like you to change some of your ways, please.

Unit 3C PAGE 16

1. **B**. The idea of a dog expressing his point of view in a letter is to entertain.
2. **A**. The humour of the letter has to do with the absurdity of a dog writing a letter—and particularly a letter asking his owners to improve their ways!
3. **B**. The list is placed after the beginning and before the ending of the letter.
4. **B**. Will's complaints are ridiculous because he is asking for the impossible.
5. **A**. You might wonder when you read the text if dogs think but this is not what the text is about.
6. **A**. Will's list mentions the notice so it is likely the dog is Will waiting patiently to get inside.
7. The new item should be written from Will's point of view and be amusing to the reader. You could write, for example, about the length of the lead when Will takes Tom and Alisa for a walk or about the rules he thinks they should follow when he lets them play ball with him!

Unit 4A PAGE 17

1. **B**. See lines 9–10.
2. **A**. See lines 10–12.
3. **C**. You can work out the photograph is of Hill Top Trine because you can see she has big hands that can be climbed into so you can get a view of the surroundings.
4. **A** and **B**. You can work out that all the giants are hidden away in out-of-the-way places that are part of the natural world: on a hill, or near a lake or stream.
5. **B**. You can work out that the idea of having the giants hidden in out-of-the-way places proved very popular. As people visited them, these places were soon better known.

6. Responses will vary. It could be argued that the most unusual thing about the sculptures is that they are hidden. Most sculptors have their work displayed in museums or at other popular sites. It is also unusual to use local volunteers but probably less unusual to use recycled materials.

Unit 4B PAGE 18

1. recycled
2. Forgotten
3. wooden
4. outstretched
5. Suggested answers: visits, visiting, visitor, visitors
6. C.
7. A.
8. used
9. recycled
10. B.
11. C.
12. hands
13. D.
14. inside her wooden body
15. they
16. You need a map to find the Forgotten Giants.
17. I climbed all over Hill Top Trine.
18. Copenhagen is the capital of Denmark.

Unit 4C PAGE 19

1. **B**. The text gives information about sculptures which are special and unusual in many ways.
2. **A**. Giants are usually big but the photo shows just how big these giants are when compared with the size of a young boy.
3. **B**. Thomas Dambo's fondness for the natural world is seen from the placing of his giants where visitors find themselves close to the natural world.
4. **C**. There is such a big difference between her name (Little) and her size (big)!
5. **A**. They all include a person's name (Trine, Louis, Tilde, Teddy) though the position of the name is not always in the same place.
6. Responses will vary. Fairytale giants are known for being powerful, cruel and terrifying. The Forgotten Giants are the opposite. They stay peacefully where they are, harming no-one and people (and birds!) can make use of them in various ways.
7. Designs will vary. To be in keeping with the other giants, the new one should be made of recycled materials and placed somewhere in the natural world.

Unit 5A PAGE 20

1. **C**. See line 17.
2. **A**. See lines 11–12.
3. **B**. You can work out that the family—Mum, Dad, Harry and Vivienne—will be celebrating Mother's Day.
4. **A** and **C**. You can work out that it will be necessary to pour the custard into the cases and add the strawberries. There is no need to turn on the oven as nothing will be cooked in it.
5. **A**. You can work out from the photograph that Harry is still quite little.
6. Responses will vary. You can judge that it is likely to be successful as everyone is doing something to please Mum. On the other hand, Harry could spill the custard and spoil the tarts!

Unit 5B PAGE 21

1. Mother's
2. tomorrow
3. spill
4. Whisk
5. Suggested answers: lucky, luckier, luckily, unluckily
6. B.
7. A.
8. bought
9. afternoon
10. D.
11. B.
12. Strawberries
13. C.
14. into a saucepan
15. he
16. It's Mother's Day tomorrow.
17. Dad says he'll be there if we need help.
18. Whisk the eggs, flour and milk together.

Unit 5C PAGE 22

1. **A**. Vivienne tells her diary what she plans to do for her mother and expresses personal thoughts and opinions.
2. **C**. The recipe tells you how to make custard.
3. **B**. Vivienne's comment about Harry is an aside. It is different from her main purpose of telling her diary about her plans.
4. **B**. Vivienne writes in her diary that they'll make the custard on Mother's Day. The photograph shows Vivienne and Harry in the process of cooking so you can infer it was taken before afternoon teatime on Mother's Day.
5. **A**. Vivienne confides her thoughts and feelings to her diary and 'talks' to it as though it were her friend.

6. Responses will vary. It suggests that the fruit and custard tarts might not turn out perfectly even with Dad's help! Both children have ingredients on themselves.
7. Responses will vary. After naming a celebration (e.g. Father's Day, a birthday, Multicultural Day) you should outline what you plan to do for your event.

Unit 6A — PAGE 23

1. **A**. See line 4.
2. **B**. See line 5.
3. **B**. You can work out that the Bully brothers usually bullied people in the park. Big Bully was worried they'd disapprove of him playing cricket instead.
4. **C**. You can work out that it was the custom of the Bully brothers to be nasty to people. Bigger Bully was angry when the ball landed near him and saw it as a chance to frighten the person responsible.
5. **B**. You can work out that Harry and Rose have invited Big Bully and Bigger Bully to play cricket with them. That means there is one more brother—Biggest Bully—left to persuade.
6. Responses will vary. You can judge that Harry and Rose hoped if they all played cricket together then the bullies might leave their bullying ways behind. The plan had worked with two of the brothers so they felt triumphant about their success.

Unit 6B — PAGE 24

1. children
2. headlong
3. sailed
4. triumphantly
5. Suggested answers: fright, frightens, frightened, frightening
6. **D**.
7. **A**.
8. skidded
9. whispered
10. **B**.
11. **C**.
12. trees
13. **B**.
14. in the park
15. It
16. "Would you like to play?" asked Harry.
17. The Bullys' house was nearby.
18. That's what happened.

Unit 6C — PAGE 25

1. **B**. A series of events tells what happened when Harry and Rosie met up with two of the Bully brothers.
2. **C**. The story is told from the outside as though someone was watching the action.
3. **C**. The reader is introduced to a threat (the bullies) at the beginning of the story; the complication occurs when part of the threat meets up with kind actions (from Harry and Rose); the resolution is a moment of triumph when good behaviour wins out over bad behaviour.
4. **B** and **C**. The amount of bullying and their sizes are reflected in their names (Big, Bigger, Biggest) but there is not a definite connection between what they eat and their names.
5. **A**. The expression of the title suggests breaking the rules of good behaviour is not playing fair.
6. Responses will vary. You can judge that it is fairly unlikely that bullying behaviour would be stopped by kind words and a smile. On the other hand, making people feel welcome and being friendly towards them may improve their behaviour.
7. Responses will vary. The next part of the story is likely to include an encounter with Biggest Bully. He might join in the cricket or he might bully everyone and break up the game proving that the best made plans don't always work out.

Unit 7A — PAGE 26

1. **C**. See line 13.
2. **B**. See line 8.
3. **B**. You can work out that, as a platypus is a monotreme and monotremes lay their eggs, a platypus must lay her eggs.
4. **A** and **B**. You can work out that having a bill which senses small movements and being able to use it to scoop up things to eat make it very useful to the platypus.
5. **C**. You can work out that semi means half (e.g. semicircle) and aquatic is to do with water (e.g. aquarium) so you can infer it means lives partly on land and partly in water.
6. Responses will vary. You can judge that it is uncommon to find an animal with several parts of its body that look like parts of other animals.

Unit 7B — PAGE 27

1. mammal
2. Scientists
3. Monotremes
4. platypus

5. Suggested answers: browner, brownest, brownish, brownness
6. C.
7. A.
8. thought
9. native
10. B.
11. D.
12. bill
13. D.
14. on a riverbank
15. It
16. The male's sting can make humans ill.
17. Its tail is like a beaver's.
18. They thought it was a trick!

Unit 7C PAGE 28

1. **B**. The text presents a file of factual information about the platypus.
2. **C**. Information about what the platypus looks like and is able to do is included but the text as a whole offers general information about the platypus.
3. **A**. The text doesn't include opinion or poetic language but some technical terms are used such as 'mammal', 'monotreme' and 'semiaquatic'.
4. **B**. The information in the brackets is an aside—a small piece of historical information —not information about the platypus.
5. **C**. The text is not about monotremes or mammals as a class. It is about one particular example of these: the duck-billed platypus.
6. Banjo Paterson compares platypuses to 'little brown billiard balls' when they are rolled up and asleep.
7. Responses will vary. Almost anything is possible! The information should relate to the body part: for example, a flipper will help it swim; large teeth will allow it to eat other animals; and so on.

NAPLAN-style Reading Test 1 PAGE 29

1. **D**. See line 4.
2. **B**. See lines 5–6.
3. **B**. Billy feels annoyed at his friends for criticising his dog and his choice of a Chihuahua.
4. **B** and **D**. Billy felt connected to Wonka from the first time he saw her and he is proud of what she can do and how she behaves.
5. **A**. To change your tune is an expression meaning to change your mind or your view about something.
6. **C**. Billy realises his friends know what he told them and they don't need to hear it again. He would be boastful rather than friendly if he said that.
7. Responses will vary. The photo shows how big the palings were for a small dog like Wonka to burrow under. Even though her task is big, she looks determined to rescue Billy and his friends. This emphasises how brave and loveable she is.

NAPLAN-style Conventions of Language Test 1 PAGE 30

1. howling
2. against
3. happened
4. listening
5. B.
6. A.
7. B.
8. C.
9. C.
10. D.
11. B.
12. C.
13. B.
14. A.

Unit 8A PAGE 31

1. **B**. See line 2.
2. **A**. See line 14.
3. **B**. You can work out that without eating at speed there is no hope the waxworms could get through the large amounts of plastic waste on our planet.
4. **A** and **C**. The good news is the hope that this discovery holds out for solutions to problems caused by plastic (i.e. the polluted environment, dead animals, and so on)
5. **A**. You can work out that there is still a question as to whether the discovery of what the waxworm can do means the plastic bag problem will be solved.
6. Responses will vary. You can judge, for example, that it is worth five stars because it is interesting news, crucial facts are given and it is told in a friendly, engaging way. Or you could judge that it is worth fewer because such an important scientific discovery should be treated more seriously.

Unit 8B PAGE 32

1. weight
2. listening
3. extremely
4. pollute
5. Suggested answers: preparing, preparation, prepared, unprepared
6. D.

7. **B.**
8. prepares
9. problem
10. **D.**
11. **B.**
12. knowledge
13. **D.**
14. yesterday morning
15. they
16. Have you read *The Very Hungry Caterpillar*?
17. That book had holes in its pages!
18. Plastic pollutes oceans, rivers and the environment.

Unit 8C — PAGE 33

1. **B.** The broadcast aims to inform people about an important scientific discovery that may help solve a serious worldwide problem.
2. **C.** The broadcast is for people generally, not just particular groups such as scientists or children.
3. **A.** The book is mentioned as a way to connect with listeners and ease into the topic by reminding them what they already know about caterpillars from their childhood reading.
4. **A** and **C.** The direct address (You're); the slang (Yikes!; Yep!) and informal language (so fingers crossed!); and the casual sentence constructions (And …; Now comes …) are evidence that the text is spoken.
5. **A.** The attitude of the speaker to her audience is friendly and warm. She assumes listeners care about the same kind of things and want news delivered in an easily understandable way.
6. **B.** You can judge that the broadcaster's attitude is hopeful about the discovery. She describes the news as good; she says the problem is worth solving; and she says to keep fingers crossed, which is a way of wishing for good luck for the project.
7. Responses will vary. The news broadcast could be more formal and serious; more jokey and trivial; longer or shorter; delivered by a male voice; include quotes from others; and so on.

Unit 9A — PAGE 34

1. **C.** See line 4.
2. **A.** See line 5.
3. **C.** You can work out that these two would be avoided because of overuse.
4. **A** and **C.** You can work out that the three animals are native to Australia and that water is the element of the platypus, air is the element of the kookaburra and land is the element of the echidna.
5. **B.** You can work out that the campaign Sid represents is about staying covered when in the sun.
6. Responses will vary. You can judge that a surfing koala is a very Australian idea; that making him different makes difference more accepted; that linking him with First Nations culture connects him to Australia's long history. Or you could argue that koalas have been overused.

Unit 9B — PAGE 35

1. Sydney
2. Olympics
3. echidna
4. Indigenous
5. Suggested answers: climbs, climbing, climber, unclimbable
6. **D.**
7. **A.**
8. said
9. campaign
10. **C.**
11. **B.**
12. luck
13. **A.**
14. in 2000
15. you (they is also possible but less likely)
16. A person, animal or thing can be a mascot.
17. In 2000, Olly was a mascot for the Olympics.
18. Sid wears shorts, a t-shirt and a hat.

Unit 9C — PAGE 36

1. **B.** The texts tells what a mascot is and describes some well-known examples.
2. **A.** The text is delivered to 3 Blue, which you can infer is a class in a school.
3. **C.** These words are a greeting. They indicate that the words are being spoken.
4. **A.** Four of the animals are linked to sporting events.
5. **C.** Popular figures in Australian culture are often given affectionate nicknames formed by shortening a name or adding an 'ie' or 'y' ending.
6. Responses will vary. As well as being a good luck symbol, mascots are used to publicise events or issues, to build a following and to arouse feelings of connection and support.
7. The talk should begin with a definition of what a mascot is and follow up with descriptions of mascots that are popular in the chosen culture.

ANSWERS

Unit 10A PAGE 37

1. **C**. See line 2.
2. **B**. See line 3.
3. **A**. You can work out that the frog loved his home and felt satisfied with what he had. He couldn't believe anywhere else was worth seeing.
4. **A** and **B**. You can work out that the birds grew tired of the frog's unwillingness to believe what they knew to be true and they found his stubborn attitude silly.
5. **C**. You can work out that at first the frog didn't believe what the birds said about the world but once he had seen it for himself, he was astonished.
6. Responses will vary. You can judge that the frog found the beauty of the world and all it had to offer a much better place to live than the narrow world of the well.

Unit 10B PAGE 38

1. insects
2. nowhere
3. attitude
4. mountains
5. Suggested answers: refuses, refused, refusing, refusal
6. **A**.
7. **B**.
8. attitude
9. exasperation
10. **C**.
11. **C**.
12. attitude
13. **D**.
14. One day
15. they
16. "Will you play with me?" asked the frog.
17. Strangely enough, he lived happily ever after.
18. "No thank you," replied the bird.

Unit 10C PAGE 39

1. **C**. This folk tale tells a story about a frog and the events that changed his life.
2. **A**. The story is told in the third person (i.e. it doesn't use 'I' or 'we'). The narrator is the teller of the tale, not a character in the story.
3. **A**. Nothing changes until the swallow takes action and removes the frog from his home.
4. **C**. The words 'Funnily enough' point out that it isn't funny at all! It may not be what the frog expected but it is what everyone else knew would happen.
5. **B**. The folk tale shows that having a closed mind may cut you off from wonderful experiences that could change your life for the better.
6. Responses will vary. The frog is content with what he has and is not envious of others. However, he doesn't have any friends and he is without goals or dreams. His worst fault is that he is stubborn and narrow-minded.
7. You may need help finding an audience. You should include all the important elements in the retelling: orientation, complication and resolution.

Unit 11A PAGE 40

1. **B**. See line 3.
2. **C**. See line 11.
3. **A**. You can work out that it is a fact that Japanese trains are very fast (e.g. the bullet trains travel at up to 320 km an hour.)
4. **B** and **C**. You can work out that the package offers a range of activities for families. This implies that it must be suitable for children and adults.
5. **A**. You can work out that the idea is placed at the end of the text to remind the viewer that if you don't act at once, you could miss out altogether.
6. Responses will vary. You can judge that the advertisement could be attractive to viewers because it emphasises family fun; has plenty of detail about the variety of activities; and puts forward convincing arguments. Or you could judge that it is unattractive because the language is exaggerated; the claims are not believable; and there is no evidence that Trend Travel is trustworthy.

Unit 11B PAGE 41

1. solution
2. breathtaking
3. island
4. scenery
5. Suggested answers: cycled, cyclist, cycling, recycle
6. **B**.
7. **C**.
8. delay
9. robotic
10. **C**.
11. **D**.
12. beauty
13. **C**.
14. in springtime
15. she
16. Fast trains, breathtaking beauty, fantastic food!
17. Will you buy the Fortnight of Fun package today?
18. Aibo, the robotic dog, is very popular.

Unit 11C PAGE 42

1. **C**. The webpage encourages people to purchase the Fortnight of Fun package from Trend Travel.
2. **C**. The emphasis in the advertisement is on the range of activities that makes it fun for families.
3. **B**. It would provide information about 'us': the people/company selling the travel package, i.e. Trend Travel.
4. **C**. You can work out that the menu heading 'Holiday packages' was bold when the site was being viewed. If the words 'Contact us' were clicked on, the site would shift to a different page and become bold.
5. **C**. It is not made clear how many parts of Japan will be visited.
6. **C**. The advertisement is cheerful in tone and doesn't try to arouse deep, heartfelt feelings.
7. Images should relate closely to the content of the website. Suitable examples include a map of Japan, a picture of Aibo, a picture of Taiko drummers, a Japanese bullet train, Japanese food, etc.

Unit 12A PAGE 43

1. **C**. See lines 2–4.
2. **B**. See line 6.
3. **C**. You can work out that items 2 and 3 are ways of getting ready for the sale and need to be done well before it starts.
4. **B** and **C**. You can work out that organising items into groups is a way of helping customers see at a glance what is for sale and where an item can be located.
5. **B**. Collecting the leftovers takes place after the sale is over and doesn't affect the sale itself.
6. Responses may vary. You can judge that Oliver is good at planning and learning from his experiences. His close attention to detail is helpful but could also be annoying. His criticism of his sisters suggests he might be a little bossy.

Unit 12B PAGE 44

1. successful
2. advertise
3. Everyone
4. quarrelled
5. Suggested answers: collects, collecting, collected, collection
6. **B**.
7. **A**.
8. local
9. display
10. **B**.
11. **D**.
12. annoyance
13. **C**.
14. at the weekend
15. it
16. We sold books, toys and clothes at our sale.
17. Everyone helped, including Mum, Dad and me.
18. The date doesn't clash with Mum's birthday, does it?

Unit 12C PAGE 45

1. **C**. Oliver lists things that should be done in order to have a good garage sale.
2. **A**. Oliver wants a guide to remind the family about what to do for a successful garage sale.
3. **B**. The action words instruct people how to do things if they want a successful garage sale.
4. **A**. The word 'rellies' is a slang word for the more formal word 'relatives'.
5. **C**. The bracketed information consists of personal comments that could be deleted without affecting the reader's understanding of what should be done.
6. Responses will vary. Oliver includes thoughtful tips that would be helpful reminders when preparing for another sale. Or it could be argued that the list could be lost and people will remember what to do anyway.
7. Responses will vary. You might include ideas such as:
   1 Send invitations out early so people keep the date free.
   2 Tell my parents about any allergies my friends have.
   3 Warn Mum and Dad in time that I'd love a birthday cake with strawberries and ice cream.

Unit 13A PAGE 46

1. **B**. See line 2.
2. **C**. See lines 6–7.
3. **B**. You can work out that the app was made as a way to give children important information about what to do in an emergency in a format that would interest them.
4. **B** and **C**. You can work out that an ambulance could take a person to hospital or a fire engine could put out a fire.
5. **A**. You can work out that it is important not to phone Triple Zero unless it is an emergency because it blocks the line for others needing urgent attention.

6. Responses will vary. You can judge that a child would need to call for help, provide information, listen carefully to advice, follow instructions and remain calm.

Unit 13B PAGE 47

1. Triple
2. emergency
3. developed
4. behaviour
5. Suggested answers: helps, helped, helping, helper
6. **D.**
7. **B.**
8. downloaded
9. immediate
10. **A.**
11. **B.**
12. emergency
13. **B.**
14. in an emergency
15. it
16. Is the Emergency+ app helpful?
17. A girl in our street was made a Triple Zero Hero.
18. What should you do in an emergency?

Unit 13C PAGE 48

1. **C.** The text is written to show what adults and children can do to be ready to deal with an emergency.
2. **A.** The writer takes a serious approach to this subject because understanding the information clearly could mean life or death for someone in the future.
3. **C.** The last line shows that children can successfully learn how to cope in emergencies so it is a goal worth following.
4. **B.** You can run an application on the internet but neither an apple nor an appetite could be run there.
5. **C.** This relates to the whole text, whereas **A** and **B** are connected to parts of the text only.
6. Responses will vary. The child should ring Triple Zero and bravely and calmly follow instructions in a serious emergency—sudden illness, fire, a dangerous situation, and so on.
7. The logo should make clear that Triple Zero is the number to call in an emergency. It could, for example, include the numbers 000, a picture of a phone or the word Emergency.

Unit 14A PAGE 49

1. **C.** See lines 2–3.
2. **B.** See lines 4–5.
3. **A.** You can work out that the land of Nod is a dream world that the poet enters when he goes to sleep.
4. **B** and **C.** You can work out that in the land of Nod the poet recognises things he sees in the real world but at the same time they are not real and disappear when he wakes up.
5. **C.** You can work out that when you are dreaming, you are by yourself. The people, places and things you see are imagined by you alone.
6. Responses will vary. You can judge that the poet is fascinated by the unusual places his dreams take him but at the same time he finds the dream world strange and a little scary.

Unit 14B PAGE 50

1. breakfast
2. through
3. frightening
4. curious
5. Suggested answers: remembers, remembering, remembered, remembrance
6. **B.**
7. **C.**
8. try
9. strangest
10. **C.**
11. **D.**
12. dreams
13. **C.**
14. every night
15. he
16. I went to the land of Nod all by myself.
17. The poem was written by RL Stevenson.
18. 'The Land of Nod' is a well-known poem.

Unit 14C PAGE 51

1. **B.** The poet is writing about what happens to him when he dreams so others can share in those experiences.
2. **B.** It would most likely be found in a book of poems as it is a poem. It is not an adventure story and doesn't tell you why people dream.
3. **A.** Without the last verse, the reader wouldn't know the poet wanted to get back into his dreams. You might think he found them too strange and frightening to return to them.
4. **B.** The rhyming of the first and second and then the third and fourth lines in every verse closely links the ideas in each pair of lines.

ANSWERS

5. **A**. Streams, mountains, things to eat and see, and frightening sights can all be found in the real world.
6. Responses will vary. You could argue that the picture suits the poem because it is of a boy asleep who could be dreaming. Yet the poet doesn't mention he takes a teddy to bed with him so you might argue that this detail means it is not such a good match.
7. Responses will vary but they must follow the rhyme scheme of aa bb. Suggested answers: I had a dream about a man / who chased his dog into a van. / I don't know if he caught his pup / because you see I then woke up.

Unit 15A PAGE 52

1. **B**. See lines 4–5.
2. **A**. See lines 7–9.
3. **A**. You can work out that as mosquitoes carry diseases it is helpful to have their numbers reduced.
4. **A** and **B**. You can work out that much could be learned from its unusually formed, powerful eyes and its extraordinarily varied flying abilities.
5. **C**. You can work out that helicopters can hover in the air, an ability that the dragonfly shares.
6. Responses will vary. You can judge that they are not alike in many ways. Nymphs are easily camouflaged, don't have wings and can't fly. Adults fly using their four wings and are not as easily camouflaged. Yet they are somewhat alike as they both eat insects and are both predatory.

Unit 15B PAGE 53

1. Dragonflies
2. surroundings
3. thousands
4. Mosquitoes
5. Suggested answers: detects, detected, detecting, detective
6. **D**.
7. **B**.
8. transparent
9. predatory
10. **D**.
11. **C**.
12. talent
13. **A**.
14. After a year or more
15. they
16. A nymph's colours blend into its surroundings.
17. It's clear that a dragonfly is a talented insect.
18. Its eyes are large and bulb-like.

Unit 15C PAGE 54

1. **C**. The text gives factual information about the dragonfly.
2. **B**. While the text does include some amazing facts about the dragonfly, it also includes more general information making it suitable for a book about insects.
3. **B**. Paragraph three is about the dragonfly's eyes so this new information should be placed here.
4. **A** and **C**. There is no information included here about its jaws or whether it is an endangered species.
5. **C**. The dragonfly is shown at rest on a twig using its legs to balance.
6. Responses will vary. Dragonflies are good hunters but they might also have many predators. Other threats might include pollution, pesticides and habitat loss. Any, or all, of these factors might reduce dragonfly numbers dramatically.
7. Generally speaking, it is estimated that dragonflies have existed for around 300 million years or more.

NAPLAN-style Reading Test 2 PAGE 55

1. **D**. See lines 6–12.
2. **C**. See lines 8–9
3. **A**, **B** and **D**. You can see in the picture that quokkas are not bald. Humans do not keep their babies in pouches so they are not marsupials.
4. **A**. The first paragraph gives general information about quokkas and their habits.
5. **B** and **C**. The presence of foxes and the failure to conserve parts of the environment inhabited by quokkas on the mainland have reduced quokka numbers there.
6. **A**. Cats don't keep their young in pouches; the other animals do.
7. Responses will vary. This text provides information about an Australian marsupial, the quokka. It could be included in an encyclopedia, a textbook or a book about Australian animals.

NAPLAN-style Conventions of Language Test 2 PAGE 56

1. furry
2. night
3. friendly
4. predator
5. **D**.
6. **C**.
7. **A**.

8. **B.**
9. **D.**
10. **A.**
11. **B.**
12. **A.**
13. **C.**
14. **C.**

Unit 16A — PAGE 57

1. **C.** See line 2.
2. **B.** See lines 3–4.
3. **A.** You can work out that several requests for less time spent at school and longer holidays add up to less time spent on lessons.
4. **A** and **C.** You can work out that Beth supports her view with a reason (they would not get their work done), as does Seamus (they wouldn't learn anything). Claudia expresses opinions but doesn't support them.
5. **B.** You can work out that Mohammed agrees with Claudia but doesn't say why.
6. Responses will vary. You can judge that the teachers might dislike Seamus's idea because lesson time would be lost or that they could approve of it because it offers a different kind of learning. They may be concerned that hobbies require expensive equipment and that finding extra teachers with the necessary expertise would be costly.

Unit 16B — PAGE 58

1. Settle
2. shouldn't
3. awful
4. photography
5. Suggested answers: learns, learning, learned, learner
6. **A.**
7. **C.**
8. disagree/don't
9. abolish
10. **D.**
11. **B.**
12. the school day
13. **C.**
14. in her bravest voice
15. **A.**
16. **B.**
17. "That's right, Year 3," said Ms Blunt.
18. "What's your opinion, Mr Kirkham?" asked Seamus.

Unit 16C — PAGE 59

1. **B.** The text looks at different points of view about a topic.
2. **A.** The students keenly contribute their comments creating a lively, pleasant atmosphere.
3. **C.** Some students give opinions without offering any good reasons for them and this lowers the standard.
4. **C.** Violet is replying to Beth's comment about wanting a uniform. She means she would never want to wear one.
5. **B.** Seamus thinks of a way to change things for the better but without going too far. His ideas may prove impractical but they keep the focus on learning.
6. **C.** The class is held outside and the students are not wearing school uniform. They all behave in a relaxed way. They do, however, take turns and speak fairly politely, which suggests there are some rules to follow.
7. Responses will vary. You could choose any aspect discussed here or introduce something different such as being allowed/not allowed to have phones in the classroom.

Unit 17A — PAGE 60

1. **B.** See line 2.
2. **C.** See line 5.
3. **B.** You can work out that having seventeen children nearby meant she always had someone to play with. She would miss that.
4. **A.** You can work out that once Casey saw how tiny and helpless Scarlet was, she felt the need to care for her.
5. **A.** You can work out that Casey's mum had taken the present with her to hospital to have it ready for Casey when she visited. She didn't want Casey to feel she'd been forgotten about.
6. Responses will vary. You can judge that Casey deals well with change. She faces the sadness or difficulties it can bring but soon lets go of the past and gets involved in what is new in her life.

Unit 17B — PAGE 61

1. memories
2. wooden
3. hospital
4. scared
5. Suggested answers: plays, played, player, playful
6. **D.**
7. **B.**
8. bouncy
9. cul-de-sac
10. **A.**
11. **C.**
12. Our new house
13. **B.**
14. very carefully
15. **D.**
16. **C.**

ANSWERS

17. On 13 September, my sister was born.
18. Did you live in a cul-de-sac?

Unit 17C PAGE 62

1. **A**. Casey tells how she thought and felt at the time of past events.
2. **C**. Notes on the fridge are usually reminders or shopping lists, not someone's special memories.
3. **C**. The first person is used to express Casey's personal, private thoughts.
4. **A**. It is likely to be fun for Casey to feel taller than everyone else and imagine herself as a giant.
5. **B**. The use of the first person makes it feel as if the reader is inside Casey, thinking as she does and learning what things feel like to her.
6. **B**. The reader is not told directly that Casey has caring parents but her reports of their actions (her mum's present; her father making her stilts) reveal their care for her.
7. Responses will vary. You could write about having a birthday, losing a tooth, getting a new brother or sister, moving house, starting school, and so on. You should write about how you thought and felt at the time.

Unit 18A PAGE 63

1. **A**. See line 1.
2. **C**. See lines 17–18.
3. **B**. You can work out that, as an Indigenous child, David lived and went to school at the Christian Mission.
4. **A** and **B**. You can work out that he proved himself through his actions and through his work with government as a worthy representative of First Australian peoples.
5. **B**. You can work out that his ideas were used but he was not paid for them. The focus of his life was not on making money.
6. Responses will vary. You can judge that David Unaipon was a man of high principles who was determined to do his best for others throughout his life. He gained everyone's respect through his selfless behaviour and many talents.

Unit 18B PAGE 64

1. continued
2. travelled
3. invention
4. design
5. Suggested answers: invents, invented, inventing, invention
6. C.
7. D.
8. favourite
9. represented
10. B.
11. A.
12. His portrait/David Unaipon
13. A.
14. on foot
15. A.
16. C.
17. He travelled far and wide, often on foot.
18. David Unaipon was a Ngarrindjeri man.

Unit 18C PAGE 65

1. **A**. The text summarises the main events in David Unaipon's life.
2. **B**. A life story of a person written by someone else is called a biography.
3. **A**. You can work out that these are David's words used to describe what he wrote about.
4. **C**. You can see from the shapes in the sketches (e.g. shearer's scissors) that they are drawings of designs for his inventions.
5. **B**. This information is in brackets as an aside. This doesn't mean it isn't an important fact, just that the author didn't emphasise it in this text.
6. Responses will vary. David always tried to help white people understand more about First Nations peoples. This was evident in his writing and his representing the views of First Australians to the government.
7. Responses will vary. You should choose an Australian who is not already included on Australian currency and who has contributed to society in worthwhile ways.

Unit 19A PAGE 66

1. **C**. See lines 3–5.
2. **C**. See lines 8–10.
3. **A**. You can work out that Mary thought stealing a few clothes didn't deserve the extremely harsh punishment of being transported for seven years.
4. **A** and **C**. You can work out that John's answers show he had a hard, unhappy life and that he was all alone with little hope of things getting any better.
5. **B**. You can work out that the stamp made to mark the journey of the First Fleet is labelled August 1787, Rio de Janeiro, a stopping place on its way.

ANSWERS

6. Responses will vary. You can judge that Mary thinks all that happened to Elizabeth and John was unfair, but that when she learns the full details of John's suffering it makes her very upset.

Unit 19B — PAGE 67

1. studying
2. stolen
3. judge
4. prisoner
5. Suggested answers: punish, punished, punishing, punisher
6. C.
7. D.
8. punishment
9. transcript
10. A.
11. B.
12. The First Fleet
13. A.
14. very upset
15. B.
16. C.
17. The *Lady Penrhyn* sailed from Portsmouth.
18. We've been learning about convicts.

Unit 19C — PAGE 68

1. **C**. This diary entry gives details about some things that happened to two young convicts.
2. **B**. Mary treats her diary as a friend she can talk easily with and as someone to whom she can tell her private thoughts and feelings.
3. **A**. An online transcript is an accurate written copy of what was said. Mary quotes words said from John's trial in the 18th century.
4. **B**. It is a friendly expression that in this context means 'I'll see you when I write in you next time.'
5. **A** and **C**. The emphasis is on splendour and celebration: a uniformed marine in the foreground; a party of well-dressed revellers playing musical instruments; a procession.
6. Responses will vary. Mary carefully records the details from her history lesson and quotes from John Hudson's actual trial at the Old Bailey. This makes it likely her information is trustworthy.
7. The conversation should include details of the life of your characters as well as of the times in which they lived.

Unit 20A — PAGE 69

1. **A**. See line 3.
2. **B**. See lines 9–10.
3. **C**. You can work out that the arrival of the ships meant the re-enactment could take place with the correct number of ships.
4. **B** and **C**. You can work out that the event's emphasis on its convict past and the date's meaning for Aboriginal Australians are likely to have concerned the government.
5. **B**. You can work out that the idea was daring and involved great challenges. As adventurers themselves, these men would have wanted to offer support.
6. Responses will vary. You can judge that the British were proud of their achievement in sailing a fleet of ships to Australia and successfully establishing a colony there. Queen Elizabeth would want to celebrate this memory.

Unit 20B — PAGE 70

1. Bicentenary
2. memorable
3. government
4. Numerous
5. Suggested answers: sail, sails, sailing, sailor
6. D.
7. B.
8. famous
9. memorable
10. D.
11. C.
12. The re-enactment/The Second First Fleet
13. B.
14. through their support for King
15. B.
16. A.
17. He crossed the Pacific Ocean on a raft.
18. There were 3000 vessels in Sydney Harbour.

Unit 20C — PAGE 71

1. **B**. The text informs its audience about the Second First Fleet.
2. **C**. The text is written rather than spoken and presents factual information rather than having people express opinions.
3. **A**. The text provides facts in a chronological sequence. The First Fleet re-enactment begins as an idea and ends as an event.
4. **A**. The brackets explain what the people named did in their lives to achieve fame.
5. **B**. Facts about the event are recorded but there is no evidence as to whether the author approves or disapproves of what happened.

6. Responses will vary. The re-enactment took place as planned and its arrival in Sydney was given a big welcome. On the other hand, not everyone approved of the project or of the money spent on it.
7. You could claim, for example, that the event was far too costly and dangerous and was an insult to Aboriginal people. Or you could point out that it provided jobs for people and was a spectacular way to celebrate an aspect of history.

Unit 21A PAGE 72

1. **B**. See lines 2 and 8.
2. **C**. See line 4.
3. **B**. You can work out that if the magnet is to be connected to the snake, the 'wall' between them must be able to be seen through.
4. **A** and **C**. You can work out that both experiments need a material that can be shaped but that also stays firm.
5. **C**. You can work out that the magnet needs to be able to swing in the direction of the magnetic pull so it must be balanced on the tip with its ends free.
6. Responses will vary. You can judge that the experiments show the magic of a magnet's powers so having the word 'fun' in the title is suitable. Or you could judge the emphasis on fun is misleading as the purpose is educational.

Unit 21B PAGE 73

1. plasticine
2. experiments
3. vertically
4. eraser
5. Suggested answers: magnetic, magnetise, magnets, magnetism
6. **C**.
7. **A**.
8. cone
9. vertically
10. **A**.
11. **C**.
12. The horseshoe magnet
13. **B**.
14. vertically without tipping.
15. **D**.
16. **C**.
17. She already had a glass jar, paper clips and a magnet.
18. You'll need some plasticine for this experiment.

Unit 21C PAGE 74

1. **C**. The text is a procedure telling you the steps to take.
2. **A**. The idea of doing the experiments is to learn more about magnets.
3. **C**. The structure of listing what you need (Ingredients) then what you should do (Method) is how recipes are organised.
4. **B**. The action verbs in this form (commands) are there to tell you what you must do step by step.
5. **C**. The author has said what should happen but leaves space for the experimenter to record what did happen.
6. Responses will vary. The picture shows a magnet drawing money to itself. It is a joke: a man thinking he has found an easy way to get rich!
7. Responses will vary. What is learnt might include: there are differently shaped magnets; magnets are attracted to, and can move, metal; the earth has a magnetic force that can attract a magnet to north or south.

Unit 22A PAGE 75

1. **C**. See line 2.
2. **B**. See line 2.
3. **B**. You can work out that to be alone and up close with a lion in a forest is a very dangerous thing.
4. **B** and **C**. You can work out that the relief of having the thorn out of his paw made the Lion feel very grateful and friendly towards Androcles.
5. **A**. You can work out that the Emperor thought Androcles's escape was a crime that earned such a punishment.
6. Responses will vary. You can judge that the Emperor was impressed by the bravery of Androcles and the faithfulness and selflessness of the Lion. He thought they had earned their freedom.

Unit 22B PAGE 76

1. groaning
2. swollen
3. Unfortunately
4. baring
5. Suggested answers: larger, largest, largish, largely
6. **D**
7. **C**
8. swollen
9. beseechingly
10. **D**.
11. **A**.
12. Androcles's hands and face
13. **C**.

14. with enjoyment
15. **A**.
16. **B**.
17. He held out his bleeding, swollen paw.
18. When he heard the story, he forgave them.

Unit 22C PAGE 77

1. **B**. The text tells an entertaining story which has a moral.
2. **C**. The narrator admires both Androcles and the Lion for their actions. The Emperor would have had Androcles killed, making him the less admirable figure.
3. **C**. It is because Androcles has helped the Lion that he spares his life at the climactic moment when it is expected he will kill Androcles.
4. **C**. By giving the word 'Lion' a capital letter, the author is separating it from lions in general. The Lion is a figure in the story with a character and personality.
5. **A**. The fable shows how trust, kindness and gratitude can make the world a better place.
6. Responses will vary. It is difficult to decide between them. Androcles's kindness and bravery, and the Lion's gratitude and loyalty, make them both worthy.
7. Responses will vary. Morals could include: a good deed will always be repaid; even the strongest may need help; good things can come in small packages.

Unit 23A PAGE 78

1. **B**. See line 4.
2. **A**. See line 2.
3. **C**. You can work out that Gretel thinks the darkness will prevent them from finding their way home.
4. **B** and **C**. You can work out that Gretel thinks they'll starve because they are without food and now it is dark they won't be able to find any.
5. **A**. You can work out that Gretel thinks Hansel has been very clever to find a way out that might save them.
6. Responses will vary. You can judge that Hansel is very good at thinking of imaginative solutions to solve his problems (e.g. the breadcrumbs, using the moon to find the right direction.) They may not always work though!

Unit 23B PAGE 79

1. breadcrumbs
2. despair
3. crescent
4. imaginary
5. Suggested answers: darker, darkest, darken, darkness
6. **B**.
7. **D**.
8. despair
9. crescent
10. **C**.
11. **B**.
12. crescent
13. **B**.
14. in despair
15. **B**.
16. **C**.
17. "You're a genius bro," Gretel said.
18. "You're right," Hansel replied.

Unit 23C PAGE 80

1. **B**. It is part of a story about two children lost in the forest.
2. **A**. You might think their stepmother wanted to be rid of the children if you have read the fairytale *Hansel and Gretel*. However, this is a different version of that story and the author does not explain why the children have been left there.
3. **B**. The extract takes place somewhere between the orientation and the resolution of the story.
4. **C**. The extract is a conversation between Hansel and Gretel so we only hear the children's points of view.
5. **B**. It is an idiom meaning you hope good luck will be with you.
6. Responses will vary. Gretel does complain and exaggerate rather a lot. But then she is in a terrible situation—lost and abandoned—so it is probably justified.
7. The ending should resolve the questions raised in the extract. For example, why the parents had left the children in the forest and whether they make it safely home.

NAPLAN-style Reading Test 3 PAGE 81

1. **C**. See line 4.
2. **A**. See line 15.
3. **A** and **D**. Plane windows are fixed and can't be opened. Nobody is allowed to get out of a plane when it is in flight as it would cause immediate death.
4. **B**. Duy is expressing his excitement to his aunt about flying by himself for the first time.

ANSWERS

5. **A** and **C**. Duy is keen to share his news with his aunt and writes to her in a warm, friendly way.
6. **B**. Duy puts the news about flying by himself in the first position in his email and emphasises how proud and pleased he is with his achievement.
7. Duy enjoyed the whole experience very much, particularly flying all by himself. It is likely that this is the part of the experience he most wants to repeat.

NAPLAN-style Conventions of Language Test 3 — PAGE 82

1. propeller (This can also be spelt propellor.)
2. enormous
3. environment
4. extremely
5. **B**.
6. **A**.
7. **C**.
8. **D**.
9. **D**.
10. **B**.
11. **B**.
12. **D**.
13. **B**.
14. **C**.

Unit 24A — PAGE 83

1. **A**. See line 6.
2. **C**. See lines 2–3.
3. **B**. You can work out that their strong legs and powerful feet make it easy for them to move about at ground level. Weak, small wings would not assist lengthy flight.
4. **A** and **C**. You can work out that it is the female who watches and listens during the male's courtship display and that both the male and the female are good mimics.
5. **B**. You can work out that the Albert's lyrebird is not mentioned.
6. Responses will vary. You can judge that it is unusual for birds to be able to copy any sound from their environment; usually they can only copy the sounds made by other birds.

Unit 24B — PAGE 84

1. fossils
2. Museum
3. muscled
4. colourful
5. Suggested answers: build, building, builder, builders
6. **B**.
7. **A**.
8. famous
9. fossils
10. **B**.
11. **C**.
12. male
13. **B**.
14. in forests to the west of the Great Dividing Range
15. **A**.
16. **A**.
17. They don't only copy sounds made by birds.
18. They can even imitate a mobile phone!

Unit 24C — PAGE 85

1. **B**. The text gives information about the lyrebird including where it lives, what it looks like and reasons for its fame.
2. **C**. As this text provides information, it could be an online encyclopedia entry in Wikipedia.
3. **A**. The word 'superb' is often used as a descriptive adjective but in this text it classifies the species of lyrebird.
4. **B**. The exclamation mark is closely linked to the last part of the sentence—the fact that this bird can imitate a mobile phone. This is a modern invention for an ancient bird to know about!
5. **A**. The text does not describe the shape or size of its tail in proportion to its body.
6. Responses will vary. The feathered tail of the male when displayed during courtship is like the shape of the lyre.
7. You should record yourself imitating any sound you can hear in the environment: other people's voices, a kookaburra laughing, a bouncing ball, and so on.

Unit 25A — PAGE 86

1. **C**. See lines 2–3.
2. **C**. See lines 12–13.
3. **B**. You can work out that the frozen water at the poles is ice that is sometimes present.
4. **A** and **B**. You can work out that the moon is made of rock and metal and has little water, which makes **A** and **B** false. It is true that the moon doesn't give out light.
5. **A**, **B** and **C**. You can work out that, without plentiful water to drink and grow crops or a suitable temperature to live in, you would not survive.
6. Responses will vary. You can judge that now man has reached the moon, there will be future expeditions where more will be learned. Technological advances may also make collecting information easier.

ANSWERS

Unit 25B PAGE 87

1. caused
2. layers
3. asteroid
4. crescent
5. Suggested answers: nightly, nightie, tonight, midnight
6. A.
7. C.
8. frozen
9. craters
10. C.
11. D.
12. further
13. C.
14. at night
15. C.
16. A.
17. Rocky objects (meteoroids and asteroids) caused the craters.
18. We learned about the moon and its qualities.

Unit 25C PAGE 88

1. C. The text provides general information about what the moon is and does.
2. B. The moon is located in space so information about it will be found in a book on that subject.
3. A. Factual details about the moon are used in this text.
4. B. Technical terms specific to the subject are used. Examples include 'craters', 'core', 'asteroids' and 'crescent'.
5. A. There is no direct mention of the moon's gravity in the text.
6. Responses will vary. The part showing treetops and the sky looks like a photograph. As there is only a single moon circling earth, the moons in the picture are drawn or superimposed onto it.
7. Jupiter has at least 67 moons and Mars has 2.

Unit 26A PAGE 89

1. C. See line 2.
2. B. See line 8.
3. A. You can work out that it is the worm's view that it is handsome, an opinion not everyone shares.
4. B and C. You can work out that the worm has no bones in its body and that it does useful work improving the soil.
5. C. You can work out that it is rare for a living thing to be able to regrow a part of itself.
6. Responses will vary. You can judge that worms are often looked down on yet they do a great deal to help humans. A medal would be justified but it would be useless to a worm, so maybe not!

Unit 26B PAGE 90

1. segment
2. handsome
3. complain
4. squirm
5. Suggested answers: newer, newest, renew, newly
6. D.
7. B.
8. recycle
9. posterior
10. C.
11. A.
12. new
13. B.
14. quickly
15. D.
16. A.
17. It's time I got a medal.
18. I'm a prize-deserving worm!

Unit 26C PAGE 91

1. A. The poem is narrated by an imaginary worm who wants to express how it feels about not being valued.
2. A and B. It is comical to hear a worm talking and some of the rhymes (e.g. work/murk; squirm/worm) add to its humour.
3. B. The worm gives reasons to prove why he deserves a medal.
4. B. The strong, regular beat makes the worm sound confident.
5. C. The worm is quite boastful about its attractiveness and good qualities. It does complain but not in a bitter way.
6. Responses will vary. The author reports facts about worms in a humorous way to persuade readers that worms deserve to be respected.
7. The new stanza should follow the rhythm, rhyme scheme and voice (first person) of the poem.

Unit 27A PAGE 92

1. C. See lines 2–3
2. B. See line 4.
3. B. You can work out that there is no information at all provided about the properties of sugar so the claim is not proven.
4. A and C. You can work out that the advertisement claims honey, when added to other foods, is tasty and that its healing properties are so famous it is now used worldwide in making bandages.

5. **A**. You can work out that the flowers are a reminder that honey comes from flower nectar, making it a natural product.
6. Responses will vary. You can judge that the word 'magical' is an exaggeration because it suggests honey has magic powers. Or you could judge that it is a fair description as honey (not just B-MADE) has such unusual and special powers.

Unit 27B PAGE 93

1. chemist
2. delicious
3. commercially
4. ancient
5. Suggested answers: uses, useful, used, unused, use-by
6. **A**.
7. **C**.
8. contains
9. nectar
10. **B**.
11. **D**.
12. use-by
13. **C**.
14. in your tea
15. **C**.
16. **A**.
17. Honey is magical!
18. Does honey have a use-by date?

Unit 27C PAGE 94

1. **B**. The text is an advertisement that aims to sell B-MADE honey.
2. **B**. The text is designed to attract buyers who value high-quality products that will improve the health of their family.
3. **A**. The advertisers present a sequence of claims about the quality of their product and promises of its benefits for the buyer.
4. **A**. All honey is made by bees and the name of the product for sale plays with that idea through its pun.
5. Responses will vary. It links the reader with the name of the honey being sold as they are both in capitals; it suggests the reader's wellbeing is the advertiser's main concern; and it implies that the work involved in making the honey is done for the personal benefit of the reader.
6. Responses will vary. Several techniques are used, such as adding emphasis through rhyme and repetition; a catchy brand name; exaggeration mixed with well-known truths to make what is said sound convincing; emotive language to persuade; personal address; and promising extraordinary benefits.
7. The advertisement should use some of the techniques identified in the answer to question 6 above.

Unit 28A PAGE 95

1. **B**. See line 2.
2. **A**. See line 14.
3. **C**. You can work out that Sanskrit is a language because it is made up of words that have meanings.
4. **A** and **B**. You can work out that silk is a luxurious, expensive material suitable for important occasions.
5. **B**. You can work out that a sari is made from material draped around the body while a kimono is cut and sewn from a pattern.
6. Responses will vary. You can judge that wearing traditional dress is a way of identifying with your own culture and representing it to others.

Unit 28B PAGE 96

1. length
2. draped
3. luxurious
4. occasions
5. Suggested answers: makes, maker, unmade, makeup
6. **C**.
7. **A**.
8. status
9. traditional
10. **B**.
11. **D**.
12. tea
13. **C**.
14. at least 3000 BCE
15. **D**.
16. **C**.
17. It has long, wide sleeves.
18. I like its colours, pattern and design.

Unit 28C PAGE 97

1. **C**. The text gives factual information about the topic of traditional dress.
2. **B**. The text includes information about the history of the sari and the kimono.
3. **B**. The text begins with information about how people have worn the kimono over time, then moves on to the way it is made and concludes with comments about what it looks like.
4. **A** and **C**. The word 'it' is used to create a reference chain with the word 'sari'. This connects the ideas and avoids unnecessary repetition.

ANSWERS

5. **A.** You can see in the picture that the kimono is hung on a rod. The sash is likely to be stored in a sleeve or elsewhere.
6. Responses will vary. Both costumes have been worn for centuries; both represent long established customs; both use images with cultural meanings.
7. The traditional casual 'uniform' for Australians is usually a sunhat, t-shirt, shorts and thongs worn by both males and females.

Unit 29A — PAGE 98

1. **C.** See lines 7–9.
2. **A.** See line 3.
3. **A.** You can work out that someone who likes his pet to cause him no effort is probably lazy.
4. **B** and **C.** You can work out that Margaret is unafraid to speak out about what she thinks and shows her caring nature in the way she looks after her pet.
5. **B.** You can work out that Margaret is ridiculing the idea that cats are cuddly.
6. Responses will vary. You can judge that nobody's arguments are completely convincing as they all say things that are hard to accept. However, the dog supporters tend to offer slightly better reasons than the cat supporters.

Unit 29B — PAGE 99

1. disagree
2. themselves
3. loyal
4. intelligent
5. Suggested answers: attends, attentive, attendance, attendant
6. **B.**
7. **C.**
8. attention
9. chaos
10. **C.**
11. **A.**
12. playful
13. **C.**
14. most days
15. **A.**
16. **A.**
17. That's my opinion.
18. They're such loyal, friendly animals.

Unit 29C — PAGE 100

1. **B.** Four people have a conversation to discuss whether cats make better pets than dogs.
2. **B.** As it is a spoken text, you would be more likely to hear it on the radio than see it printed anywhere.
3. **B.** The comments are part of a conversation where people respond one to the other.
4. **C.** You would expect it to be stated in the opening sentence but it is only given in the title.
5. **A.** Margaret says this sincerely. The inverted commas show she means that her dog communicates with her rather than literally talks to her.
6. Responses will vary. The caption will probably have the animals making a comment such as "You're all talking nonsense!" or the dog could be saying "Now, listen here!".
7. Responses will vary. Comments should contain convincing reasons or evidence rather than unsupported claims and opinions.

Unit 30A — PAGE 101

1. **B.** See line 1.
2. **B.** See line 4.
3. **C.** You can work out that fighting in the war divided people into friends and enemies. After the war was over, his family's lives were still at risk.
4. **A** and **C.** You can work out that there were many who had enemies and needed to escape. The boats available risked taking more than they should to fit everyone in.
5. **B.** You can work out that one reason Brad admires Anh Do is for his generosity in giving away money to people who need help.
6. Responses will vary. You can judge that when Anh Do's family reached Australia they would, for example, have to find a place to live, earn money to support the family, find new friends and learn a new language.

Unit 30B — PAGE 102

1. Vietnamese
2. Thieving
3. Eventually
4. profits
5. Suggested answers: dangerous, dangerously, endanger, endangered
6. **C.**
7. **D.**
8. overcome
9. hero
10. **C.**
11. **D.**
12. true
13. **B.**
14. with others in a crowded boat
15. **B.**

ANSWERS

16. **B**.

17. Anh Do is my new hero!

18. The book's profits were given to a charity.

Unit 30C PAGE 103

1. **C**. The text is a review of the book, *The Little Refugee*, written by Brad.
2. **A**, **B** and **C**. Brad's review would be helpful for other children looking for a book to interest them. Parents and librarians who choose books for children would also find it helpful to see what a child aged nine enjoys reading.
3. **B**. Paragraph two summarises the adventures that happen on the boat journey as reported by Anh Do.
4. **A**. Anh Do tells the story of what really happened in the early part of his life.
5. **A**. It is Anh Do's tone of voice and the way he talks directly to the reader that makes Brad feel close to him.
6. Responses will vary. It is related to the idea of children enjoying reading books rather than the particular book that is reviewed.
7. Responses will vary. At 14, Anh Do started a small business selling tropical fish; he studied law at University; he became a stand-up comedian instead of a lawyer; he bought his mum a house; he became an author. He has also hosted TV shows and performed popular stage shows.

NAPLAN-style Reading Test 4 PAGE 104

1. **B**. See line 6.
2. **C**. See lines 14–15.
3. **B**. This is an advertisement for The Fitters. It is trying to entice more people to join the group and pay the membership fees.
4. **B**, **C** and **D**. Advertisements are not included in encyclopedias but could appear in the other places.
5. **A**. Including handwritten comments is a way for advertisers to stress that real people such as Ally and Bill personally have said good things about The Fitters.
6. **D**. Ally may have got into the football team anyway. It sounds as if she was fit already.
7. Responses will vary. The advertisement aims to appeal to a wide range of people and the information is well organised. On the other hand, the proof of the group's effectiveness is not very convincing and the cost is not revealed.

NAPLAN-style Conventions of Language Test 4 PAGE 105

1. exercise
2. disappeared
3. Eventually
4. February
5. B.
6. A.
7. B.
8. D.
9. C.
10. D.
11. A.
12. B.
13. D.
14. C.

ANSWERS

NOTES

NOTES

Updated in 2023 for the NSW Curriculum and Australian Curriculum Version 9.0 changes

Reprinted 2025

ISBN 978 1 74125 649 9

Pascal Press
PO Box 250
Glebe NSW 2037
www.pascalpress.com.au

Publisher: Vivienne Joannou
Project editor: Mark Dixon
Edited and proofread by Mark Dixon
Answers checked by Dale Little
Cover and page design by Sonia Woo
Typeset by Grizzly Graphics (Leanne Richters)
Printed by Vivar Printing/Green Giant Press